Sunset
Food
Processor
COOK BOOK

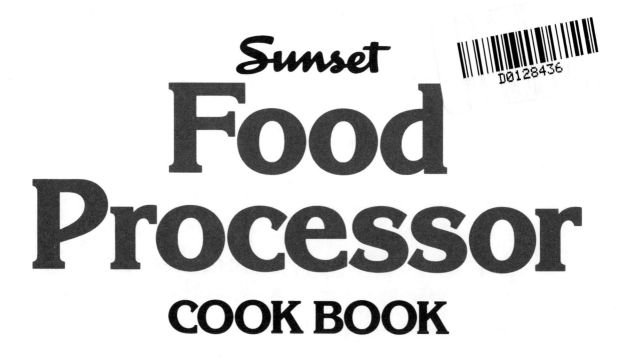

By the Editors of Sunset Books
and Sunset Magazine

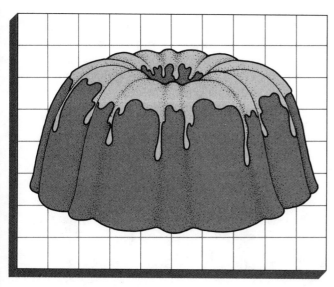

Lane Publishing Co. • Menlo Park, California

Research & Text
Elizabeth Friedman

Coordinating Editor
Cornelia Fogle

Special Consultant
Joan Griffiths

Design
Joe di Chiarro

Illustrations
Sally Shimizu

Photography
Victor Budnik

Photo Editor
Lynne B. Morrall

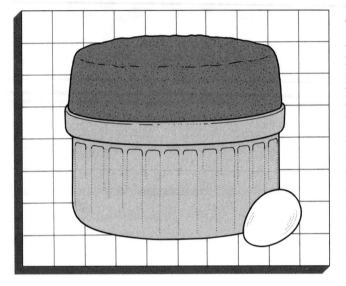

Cover: The city of Naples is perhaps best known for its culinary contribution to the rest of the world—pizza. Here, we feature a fresh and colorful version of this perennial favorite, with sliced mushrooms, red bell peppers, pepperoni, and jack cheese layered on a base of herbed tomato sauce. From dough to toppings, all ingredients are prepared in the food processor. The recipe for Mushroom-Pepperoni Pizza is on page 82. Photography by Nikolay Zurek. Cover design by Lynne B. Morrall.

Editor, Sunset Books: David E. Clark

First printing April 1985

A Tool for Good Cooking

A welcome addition to any kitchen, the food processor streamlines preparation of all your favorite dishes. In fact, we predict that once you've grown accustomed to using it, you'll wonder how you ever got along without one. With the help of your processor, you'll master the most fundamental kitchen duties and the most sophisticated techniques with equal ease and efficiency: making fresh pasta or yeast dough, French *quenelles*, and extravagant, show-stopping desserts is just as simple and speedy as chopping an onion, shredding cheese, or slicing carrots.

All food processors come with at least three basic attachments: a metal blade, a slicing disc, and a shredding disc. In the charts beginning on page 8 and in the introductions to our recipes, we've used the following illustrations to call out the particular blades needed for performing a procedure or preparing a recipe.

Metal blade   Slicing disc   Shredding disc

Whether you've owned a processor for years or have yet to take it out of the box, you'll enjoy using the ideas, recipes, and techniques in this book. All were designed to let the processor do all the work; you just collect the compliments when diners taste the results.

Our special thanks to Rebecca LaBrum for her thorough editing of the manuscript. We also thank Best of All Worlds, Brown's China & Glass, House of Today, Peninsula Plating Works, Rorke's, S. Christian of Copenhagen, Taylor & Ng, William Ober Co., and Williams-Sonoma Kitchenware for their generosity in sharing props for use in photographs.

Contents

Processing Techniques

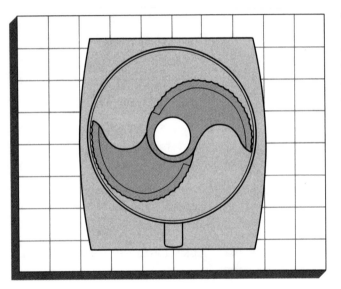

The food processor is a proven boon to all cooks—to those who cook for sheer enjoyment as well as those who race the clock to hurry dinner to the table. Whether your cooking is simple or sophisticated, the processor can help you prepare high-quality fresh ingredients with lightning speed.

Since their introduction over a decade ago, food processors have come a long way. Design and function of all brands have improved, so much so that the original machines look antiquated next to the latest models. Many of the newer processors have larger, more powerful motors, which propel an extra-large work bowl's worth of ingredients with ease. Blades and discs have also become more refined and specialized.

Whether you've owned a processor for years or have yet to take it out of the box, whether your particular model is souped up or stripped down, you'll enjoy using the following techniques and recipes to prepare all manner of foods. You'll find soups and salads, appetizers, hearty main courses, and luscious desserts—all easy to make in record time with the food processor.

The Processor

A food processor can be an invaluable addition to any kitchen. But like most other tools, it will serve you best if you understand how it works.

Mechanics. The processor's motor is encased in a sturdy plastic base. In most models, the motor is directly below the work bowl (direct drive assembly); in a few others, it's behind or beside the bowl (belt-driven assembly). Direct drive is considered superior because, as the name implies, it provides a more direct and hence more efficient transfer of power from motor to blade.

A metal shaft extends from the base through the center of the work bowl, connecting blades and discs to the motor. When the bowl is locked into place and the motor is switched on, the shaft turns, propelling blades and discs. Most models have "on," "off," and "pulse" buttons or switches on the base to control the processing action.

Work bowls & covers. Both work bowls and covers are made of clear, heat-resistant plastic; most are dishwasher safe (check manufacturer's instructions). Many bowls have built-in handles. Some models also have *continuous feed*—a chute off the side of the bowl that opens to empty the bowl as it fills. If your processor has this feature, you can slice or shred a large quantity of food without having to empty the bowl.

All covers have a feed tube—a chimneylike chute that both holds foods to be sliced or shredded and provides an easy way to add ingredients to the work bowl while the motor is running. A removable plastic piece called a pusher fits into the feed tube; it guides foods safely down the tube for slicing or shredding, and also contains spatters when you're chopping, mixing, or puréeing. Some covers, particularly those on early-model machines, double as on-off switches.

In recent years, manufacturers have introduced optional covers with large feed tubes. These proved so popular that some companies no longer produce processors with standard feed tubes. Large feed tubes reduce the preparation needed to slice or shred food: while an apple must be halved or quartered to fit a standard tube, a large tube can contain the whole fruit.

As feed tubes have grown, so has the rest of the machine. The first processors came with 4-cup bowls; today, you'll find models that hold 6, 8, or 10 cups—or even a full gallon. These bigger machines have correspondingly larger, more powerful motors, and can handle chores unheard of when processors were introduced: they can easily knead large batches of yeast dough or grind more than a pound of meat at once. At the same time, the largest processor can still mince a single clove of garlic as efficiently as the smallest.

Blades & Discs

All food processors come with at least three cutting attachments: a metal blade, a slicing disc, and a shredding disc. In the charts on pages 8 to 15 and in our recipes, these are represented by the following symbols:

Metal blade   Slicing disc   Shredding disc

Some processors also include a plastic blade; its recommended functions vary depending on the manufacturer.

Metal blade. The metal blade performs a host of chores—chopping, mincing, blending, puréeing, and mixing—so it's no surprise that most processor cooks use this attachment far more than any other. The S-shaped blade is made of stainless steel, with cutting edges on both sides; a plastic knob in the center makes insertion and removal easy. The blade is designed to chop for years and years without sharpening. When it has finally dulled to the point of inefficiency, manufacturers recommend replacing rather than sharpening it; some will do this for a reduced charge.

Success in working with the metal blade lies in understanding the timing and techniques involved. For smooth, even-textured mixtures such as sauces, crumbs, and purées, simply let the motor run continuously until the desired texture is achieved. But when you want to retain distinct pieces (as in chopping vegetables, for example), it's essential to use on-off pulses.

An on-off pulse is defined as the time required to depress, then immediately let up on the "pulse" button (or to turn the cover to the "on" position, then immediately back to "off"). This action allows you to control the speed with which the blade turns. It also moves food more efficiently around the work bowl: each time the motor stops, the food drops to the bottom of the bowl, so it will be in the path of the blade when the motor starts up again. Train yourself to think "off" as soon as you think "on." Bear in mind that it's always possible to process something a little further if it's not fine enough, but it's impossible to correct something that's been overprocessed.

Plastic blade. This white plastic duplicate of the metal blade was originally designed to blend soft mixtures, but consumers found it more convenient to use the metal blade for everything.

In response, some manufacturers have discontinued the plastic blade; others have designed a new one specifically for kneading yeast dough. Still others continue to manufacture the original. If your processor has a plastic blade, be sure to use it as the manufacturer recommends.

Slicing & shredding discs. These two discs spin level with the top of the work bowl. The techniques used for slicing and shredding are almost identical—food to be sliced or shredded is loaded into the feed tube and supported on the bottom by the disc.

Standard slicing discs cut slices approximately 3 to 4 millimeters (about ⅛ to ⅙ inch) thick; standard shredding discs produce even shreds about 6 millimeters (¼ inch) wide.

Accessory discs. A number of accessory discs are available from several manufacturers. Extra-thick slicers cut hefty slices (up to 8 millimeters thick) for sandwich toppings; extra-thin slicers—some as narrow as 1 millimeter—make exquisite paper-thin slices for salads or garnishes. With the aid of a fine shredder, you can also make extra-thin, delicate shreds. More sophisticated still is the French fry disc, available for several processor models; it cuts potatoes and other vegetables into ridged sticks. Finally, there are a few special discs that make julienne strips (matchstick pieces).

A Tool for Good Cooking

Though it can't transform you into a master chef overnight, a food processor may very well renew your enthusiasm for cooking—it streamlines the tedious preparation that often deters cooks from trying new culinary styles.

New Techniques & Recipes

When food processors were introduced, their strengths were thought to be limited to chopping, shredding cheese, and puréeing. We now know that they can do much, much more. Our techniques and recipes will teach you how to make sophisticated cuts with standard equipment, knead yeast dough to perfection, and beat egg whites for soufflés or mousses.

We've tested our recipes over and over, in a variety of machines—small and large, old and new. We're confident that you'll get perfect results when you cook from this book—and when you use our techniques to adapt your own recipes.

Safety & Convenience

To get the safest, most effective service from your machine, keep these common-sense rules in mind each time you use your processor.

• Before operating your processor for the first time, read the instruction manual thoroughly to familiarize yourself with the machine's parts, use, and care. Capabilities vary from one machine to another; let the manufacturer's instructions be the final word for your particular model.

• Handle the metal blade and discs with as much respect as you'd handle a knife: the cutting edges are razor sharp. Be sure to store blades out of reach of children.

• *Never* insert any blade until the work bowl is locked in place. After inserting a blade or disc, be sure it's down as far as possible on the shaft.

• *Always* use the pusher when slicing or shredding. *Never* put your fingers in the feed tube.

• *Always* wait for the metal blade or a disc to stop spinning before you remove the cover.

• When chopping food, insert the metal blade before adding food to the work bowl. This is easy to forget at first. Putting food in first won't cause any damage, but it's a nuisance to empty out the bowl, fit in the blade, and start again.

• To empty the work bowl filled with dry ingredients, remove the blade first or hold it in place with your fingers as you tip the bowl upside down. (Or, if the work bowl has a hole in the bottom, put one finger in it, then invert the bowl. The blade will stay firmly in place.)

• To empty the work bowl filled with liquid, hold the blade in place against the bottom of the bowl with a spatula or your hand. This prevents leakage and stops the blade from dropping out and cutting you. To clean the last bit of a liquid mixture off the metal blade, replace the empty work bowl (with blade in place) on the base; put on the cover and turn on the machine for just a few seconds. The blade will be clean, and the remaining liquid mixture can be easily and neatly scraped off the sides of the bowl.

• *Never* leave the metal blade soaking in soapy water, planning to return and wash it later. You may forget it's there and be unable to see the sharp edges through the suds. It's best to wash the blade right after using it.

• A food processor is built with a temperature-controlled circuit breaker that automatically cuts off the current if a machine overheats from mixing a load that's too heavy. If your machine stops, turn it off, then wait the length of time recommended in your manual before starting it again.

PARTS OF A FOOD PROCESSOR

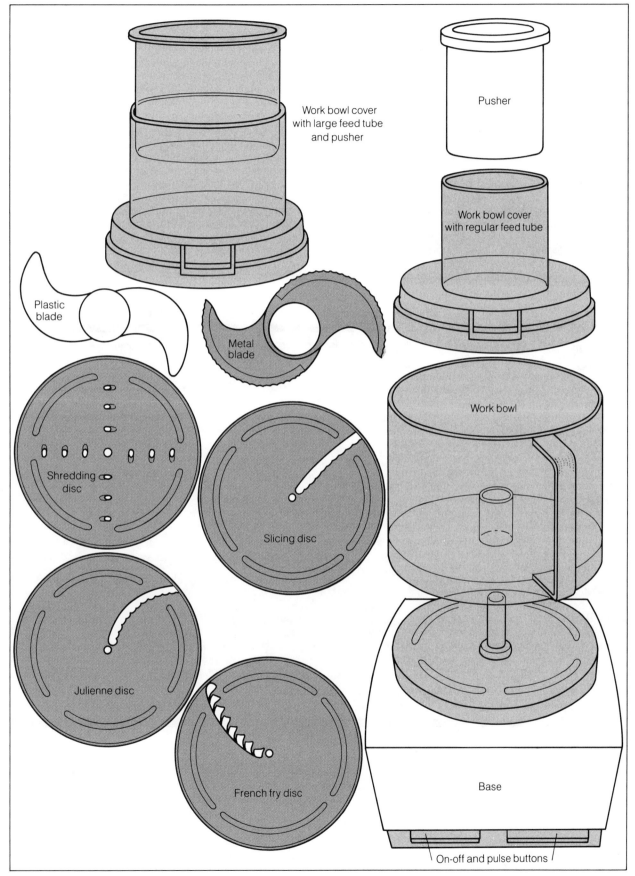

Work bowl cover with large feed tube and pusher

Pusher

Work bowl cover with regular feed tube

Plastic blade

Metal blade

Work bowl

Shredding disc

Slicing disc

Julienne disc

French fry disc

Base

On-off and pulse buttons

FOOD PROCESSING TECHNIQUES

The guidelines in the following charts will help you get the best results from your processor. Look here for recommendations on the most appropriate processing size, temperature, and positioning for various foods, and for details on the best processing methods for each. You'll find these charts a handy guide whether you're cooking from our recipes or from your own.

NOTE: Suggestions for filling the work bowl are based on standard machines with a 4-cup capacity. If you have a large-capacity processor, follow manufacturer's instructions for maximum amounts to process at one time.

When slicing or shredding, *always empty the bowl when food reaches the fill line.*

Chart Key

Metal blade   Slicing disc   Shredding disc

Dairy Products & Eggs

Special tips. Temperature is important when working with cheeses. *Firm and semisoft cheeses* process best when cold, so use them directly from the refrigerator. Before processing *hard cheeses*, bring them to room temperature, then check firmness with the following **knife test:** insert a thin knife into the cheese; it should easily penetrate ¼ to ½ inch. If it doesn't, the cheese is too hard and may harm the machine—you should grate it by hand.

Whipping cream can be beaten in the processor, but it won't look as fluffy or have as great a volume as cream beaten with a whisk or an electric mixer.

Food/Amount	Form/Blade	Basic Preparation	Processing Procedure/Yield
Cheese, firm or semisoft (Cheddar, jack, Swiss, etc.) *1 pound*	Shredded	Use directly from refrigerator. Cut off and discard any rind. Cut to fit feed tube.	Place in feed tube; shred. Yield: 4 cups.
Cheese, hard (Parmesan, Romano, etc.) *5 ounces*	Grated	Bring to room temperature. Check firmness with the knife test (see "Special tips," above). Cut off and discard rind; cut cheese into 1-inch chunks.	With motor running, drop cheese through feed tube, a few chunks at a time; continue processing until as fine as desired (see photo on page 11). Yield: 1 cup.
Eggs, hard-cooked *up to 8 eggs*	Chopped	Peel. If chopping more than 4 eggs, cut in half crosswise.	Place in work bowl. Chop, using on-off pulses, until as fine as desired. Yield: 1 egg = about ⅓ cup.
Whipping cream *1 cup*	Thickened	Use directly from refrigerator.	Pour into work bowl; process continuously until thick (see photo on page 11). Yield: 1½ cups.

Fruits

Special tips. Firm-ripe fruits give the best results in the food processor. You'll almost always get a few unevenly cut pieces, though; if you want fruit that's sliced or chopped perfectly evenly, use a knife. (For more details on slicing, see "Tips for Slicing," page 37.)

Some fruits, such as apples, bananas, nectarines, peaches, and pears, turn brown when cut and exposed to air. If you won't be using these fruits immediately after processing, sprinkle them with lemon juice to prevent browning.

Food/Amount	Form/Blade	Basic Preparation	Processing Procedure/Yield
Apples *1 pound* (about 3 small)	Sliced	Peel if desired; cut into quarters and core.	Stack quarters in feed tube as shown on page 11. Slice. Yield: 3 to 3½ cups.
	Chopped	Prepare as directed above.	Place up to half of pieces at a time in work bowl; chop, using on-off pulses, until as fine as desired. Yield: 3 to 3½ cups.
Bananas *1 pound* (2 medium-size)	Sliced	Peel; cut into lengths to fit vertically in feed tube.	Pack vertically in feed tube, cut ends down. Slice, using light pressure with pusher. Yield: 1½ to 2 cups.

Food/Amount	Form/Blade	Basic Preparation	Processing Procedure/Yield
Candied or pitted dried fruit *up to 2 cups*	Chopped	Reserve about ¼ cup sugar or flour from recipe for each ½ cup fruit.	Place fruit and sugar or flour in work bowl. Chop, using on-off pulses, until as fine as desired. Yield: ½ cup fruit plus ¼ cup flour or sugar = ½ cup chopped fruit.
Citrus fruit *1 small lemon, 1 medium-size lime, or 1 medium-size orange*	Sliced	For best results, choose fruit which fits tightly in bottom of feed tube. (See photo on page 11.) Trim a small slice from each end. If fruit is too large to fit through bottom of feed tube, cut in half lengthwise.	Insert vertically through bottom of feed tube. Place cover over slicing disc; slice. If using halved fruit, don't stack halves; slice each separately. Yield: 1 small lemon = about ½ cup; 1 medium-size lime = about ½ cup; 1 medium-size orange = about 1 cup.
Coconut *1¼ to 1½ pounds*	Shredded	Pierce eyes; drain off milk. Place coconut in a shallow baking pan. Bake in a 350° oven for 30 minutes. Let cool. Hold coconut on a hard surface and hit with a hammer; separate flesh from shell with a screwdriver. Pare off brown skin, if desired; cut pieces to fit feed tube.	Pack in feed tube; shred. (Lift pusher slightly if coconut sticks.) Yield: about 4½ cups.
Peaches or nectarines *1 pound (3 medium-size)*	Sliced	Peel if desired; cut into quarters and remove pit.	Process as directed for Apples, sliced; use light pressure with pusher. Yield: 2½ to 3 cups.
Pears *1 pound (about 3 small)*	Sliced	For lengthwise slices, use small pears (ends trimmed, if necessary, to fit in feed tube). Peel if desired, cut into quarters, and core.	For lengthwise slices, pack pear quarters horizontally in feed tube, flat side down; slice. For crosswise slices, stack vertically in feed tube, alternating thick and thin ends; slice. Yield: about 3 cups.
Pineapple *3 pounds (1 small)*	Chopped	Trim ends of pineapple; then peel, remove eyes, cut into quarters, and core. Cut cored quarters into 1½-inch chunks.	Place up to half of pieces at a time in work bowl; chop, using on-off pulses, until as fine as desired. Yield: about 2½ cups.
Strawberries *1 pound (about 3 cups)*	Sliced	Hull.	Stack horizontally in feed tube; slice, using very light pressure with pusher. Yield: about 2¼ cups.

Meats & Poultry

Special tips. The secret to evenly sliced raw meat and poultry is to freeze it to the right consistency—too little freezing and meat will be too soft to slice evenly, too much and it could be hard enough to damage the slicing disc or motor. We find it easiest to freeze meat overnight or longer, then thaw it just enough to pass the **knife test** (about 1½ hours at room temperature for 1 pound of meat). Insert a thin knife into center of meat; it should easily penetrate ¼ to ½ inch (see photo on page 11). If it doesn't, meat is too hard and may harm the machine—thaw it further or slice by hand.

Before chopping or grinding meat or poultry, remove any bones, connective fibers, and gristle; these could damage the metal blade. Trim heavy outside fat from meat; leave small pieces of inside fat for juiciness and flavor, if desired.

Food/Amount	Form/Blade	Basic Preparation	Processing Procedure/Yield
Beef, cooked *1 pound boneless (3 cups chunks)*	Chopped/ground	Use any cut which has been barbecued, broiled, roasted, or pan-fried. Use at room or refrigerator temperature. Trim any connective fibers, gristle, and excess fat. Cut into 1-inch chunks.	Place up to ¾ pound at a time in work bowl. Chop, using on-off pulses, until as fine as desired. Yield: 4 servings.
Beef, raw *1 pound boneless*	Sliced	Choose top round or sirloin. Trim any connective fibers, gristle, and excess fat. Cut with grain into lengths to fit vertically in feed tube. Wrap and freeze until firm, then partially thaw (meat must pass the knife test—see "Special tips," above).	Tightly pack vertically in feed tube; slice. Yield: 4 servings.

(Continued on next page)

Food/Amount	Form/Blade	Basic Preparation	Processing Procedure/Yield
Beef, raw *1 pound* *boneless*	Chopped/ground	Choose chuck, round, sirloin, or lean stew meat. Use at refrigerator temperature. Trim any connective fibers, gristle, and excess fat. Cut into 1-inch chunks.	Place up to ¾ pound at a time in work bowl. Chop, using on-off pulses, until as fine as desired. Yield: 4 servings.
Chicken, cooked *1 pound* *boneless* *(3 cups chunks)*	Chopped/ground	Use light or dark meat, at room or refrigerator temperature. Remove skin and fat; cut meat into 1-inch chunks.	Place up to ¾ pound at a time in work bowl; chop, using on-off pulses, until as fine as desired. Yield: 4 servings.
Chicken, raw, breast only *1 pound* *boneless*	Sliced	Use a whole boned breast, skinned and split. Wrap and freeze until firm, then partially thaw (meat must pass the knife test—see "Special tips," page 9).	Tightly pack both breast halves vertically in feed tube; slice. Yield: 4 servings.
Ham, cooked *1 pound* *boneless* *(3 cups chunks)*	Chopped/ground	Use at room or refrigerator temperature. Trim any gristle and excess fat. Cut into 1-inch chunks.	Place up to ¾ pound at a time in work bowl; chop, using on-off pulses, until as fine as desired. Yield: 4 servings.
Lamb, raw *1 pound* *boneless*	Chopped/ground	Choose lean shoulder or stew meat. Use at refrigerator temperature. Trim any connective fibers, gristle, and excess fat. Cut into 1-inch chunks.	Place up to ¾ pound at a time in work bowl; chop, using on-off pulses, until as fine as desired. Yield: 4 servings.
Pork, raw *1 pound* *boneless*	Sliced	Choose tenderloin (or buy loin or rib chops and bone). Prepare as directed for Beef, raw (sliced).	Tightly pack vertically in feed tube; slice. Yield: 4 servings.
	Chopped/ground	Choose shoulder or butt. Prepare as directed for Lamb, raw.	Place up to ¾ pound at a time in work bowl; chop, using on-off pulses, until as fine as desired. Yield: 4 servings.
Sausage, firm, fully cooked (such as bratwurst, kielbasa, and frankfurters) *1 pound*	Sliced	Use at refrigerator temperature. Cut into lengths to fit vertically in feed tube. (For neater firm sausage slices, freeze for 45 minutes before processing.)	Tightly pack vertically in feed tube, cut ends down. Slice. Yield: 4 servings.

Miscellaneous

Special tips. Nuts can be chopped quickly and easily in the food processor, but will turn to nut butter if processed for too long. (Directions for making flavorful nut butters are on page 96.) Always use on-off pulses to chop nuts, and stop the machine frequently to check fineness.

Grating chocolate with the shredding disc gives the most even results, but this method isn't recommended for all machines or all models. Be sure to check the manufacturer's instructions for your processor before you start to grate.

Food/Amount	Form/Blade	Basic Preparation	Processing Procedure/Yield
Bread, dry or soft *Up to 5 slices*	Crumbs	Break or tear into quarters.	Place in work bowl. Process continuously until as fine as desired. Yield: 1 slice bread = ¼ cup dry crumbs, ½ cup soft crumbs.
Chocolate (all types) *1 ounce*	Grated	Check manufacturer's instructions (see "Special tips," above). Fairly thick pieces process most evenly; chill all types but unsweetened before processing.	Place in feed tube. Grate, using firm pressure with pusher (see photo on page 11). Yield: 3 tablespoons.
Cookies *20 chocolate* *or 24 vanilla* *wafers*	Crumbs	No preparation needed.	Place in work bowl. Process continuously until as fine as desired. Yield: about 1 cup.

(Continued on page 12)

Processor Basics

Process chocolate in 1 of 2 ways: either grate with shredding disc or chop with metal blade. Grating produces more even results, but may harm your machine (check manufacturer's recommendations).

To slice apples, core peeled or unpeeled quarters; then stack quarters in feed tube, with cored sides facing each other. Slice.

To slice citrus fruit, cut a piece from bottom so fruit lies flat against disc. If fit is snug, ease fruit into bottom of feed tube from underneath cover.

Always check texture of meat before slicing. Partially thaw frozen meat (or poultry) as directed on page 9. Then try the knife test: if tip easily penetrates ¼ to ½ inch, slice as directed on pages 9 and 10.

To thicken cream, pour refrigerator-temperature whipping cream into work bowl; process continuously until thickened (cream will not be light and fluffy like whipped cream).

To grate Parmesan cheese, bring cheese to room temperature; then check hardness with a knife (see page 8). Cut into chunks about 1 inch square. With motor running, drop chunks through feed tube.

Food/Amount	Form/Blade	Basic Preparation	Processing Procedure/Yield
Crackers *28 saltines or 16 graham squares*	Crumbs	No preparation needed.	Place in work bowl; process continuously until as fine as desired. Yield: about 1 cup.
Nuts all varieties *1 cup shelled*	Chopped	No preparation needed.	Place in work bowl. Chop, using on-off pulses, until as fine as desired. Yield: about 1 cup.

Vegetables

Special tips. For best results, use produce that's firm and crisp. It's normal to get a few unevenly cut pieces; if you want perfectly cut pieces, use a knife. (For more details on slicing, see "Tips for Slicing," page 37.)

To shred just one long vegetable (such as a carrot) or slice it crosswise, cut it into 2 or 3 even lengths, or enough to fit snugly when packed vertically in the feed tube.

We give directions for making julienne strips by cutting vegetables twice with the slicing disc. If you have a French fry disc or one that produces julienne strips, follow the manufacturer's instructions.

For information on puréeing vegetables, see page 46.

Food/Amount	Form/Blade	Basic Preparation	Processing Procedure/Yield
Beans, green, Italian, or wax *1 pound*	French-cut	Trim ends; cut beans into lengths to fit horizontally in feed tube.	Stack horizontally in feed tube; slice (see photo on page 14). Yield: about 4 cups.
Beets, cooked *1 pound* *(4 or 5 small)*	Sliced	Trim stem and root ends; peel. If beets are too large to fit in feed tube, cut in half lengthwise.	Insert one beet through bottom of feed tube. Place cover over slicing disc; pack tube with more beets. Slice. Yield: about 2½ cups.
	Shredded	Prepare as directed above.	Stack in feed tube; shred. Yield: about 2½ cups.
Cabbage, green, red, or napa *1 pound* *(1 small head)*	Shredded	Core; cut lengthwise into quarters or eighths to fit vertically in feed tube.	Pack vertically in feed tube; shred using slicing disc (see photo on page 14). Yield: green or red = about 5 cups, lightly packed; napa = about 6 cups, lightly packed.
	Chopped	Core; cut lengthwise into quarters, then crosswise into 2-inch chunks.	Place up to half of pieces at a time in work bowl; chop, using on-off pulses, until as fine as desired. Yield: about 4½ cups, lightly packed.
Carrots *1 pound* *(3 or 4 medium-size)*	Sliced	Trim ends; peel if desired. Cut into lengths to fit vertically in feed tube.	Pack vertically in feed tube, alternating thick and thin ends; slice. Yield: about 3½ cups.
	Julienne strips	Trim ends; peel if desired. Cut into lengths to fit horizontally in feed tube. (Technique for cutting julienne strips is pictured on page 14 for zucchini.)	Pack horizontally in feed tube, alternating thick and thin ends; slice. Stack slices; turn stack on its side, long, thin edges down. Tightly fit stack into bottom of feed tube with pusher in place (hold cover at an angle so carrots don't fall out). Carefully place cover over disc and slice. (Process one stack at a time.) Yield: about 3½ cups.
	Shredded	Trim ends; peel if desired. Cut into lengths to fit vertically in feed tube.	Pack vertically in feed tube, alternating thick and thin ends; shred. Yield: about 4 cups lightly packed.
Celery *3 large stalks*	Sliced	Trim ends; remove strings, if desired. Cut into lengths to fit vertically in feed tube.	Nest curved part of stalks together; pack vertically in feed tube. Slice. Yield: about 2 cups.
	Chopped	Trim ends; cut into 1½-inch lengths.	Place in work bowl; chop, using on-off pulses, until as fine as desired. Yield: about 2 cups.

Food/Amount	Form/Blade	Basic Preparation	Processing Procedure/Yield
Celery root 1 pound (1 small)	Sliced	Trim ends, peel, and cut into quarters lengthwise to fit vertically in feed tube.	Pack in feed tube; slice. Use, or place in lemon water (3 tablespoons lemon juice to 4 cups water) to prevent browning. Yield: 4 cups.
	Julienne strips	Prepare as directed above. (Technique for cutting julienne strips is pictured on page 14 for zucchini.)	Slice as directed above. Stack slices, then turn stack on its side—thin, flat edges down. Continue as directed for Carrots, julienne strips. (If feed tube is large, place 2 stacks side by side). Slice; use, or submerge in lemon water (see above). Yield: about 3½ cups.
Cucumber 1 small	Sliced	Trim ends; peel or score if desired. Cut into lengths to fit vertically in feed tube.	Place vertically in feed tube, cut end down; slice. Yield: about 1¼ cups.
Fennel 1 pound (1 medium-size bulb)	Sliced	Trim stalks just above bulb; trim bulb base. Cut bulb in half lengthwise; trim sides, if necessary, to fit vertically in feed tube.	Place vertically in feed tube; slice. Yield: about 4 cups.
Garlic up to 1 head	Minced	Separate into cloves; peel cloves.	With motor running, drop through feed tube, one clove at a time; continue processing until minced. Yield: 1 large clove = 1 teaspoon.
Ginger, fresh 1 by 1-inch piece	Chopped or minced	Peel if desired; cut into quarters.	With motor running, drop through feed tube; continue processing until as fine as desired. Yield: about 2 tablespoons.
Herbs		*See* Parsley.	
Jicama 1 pound (1 small)	Shredded	Trim ends; peel. Trim sides, if necessary, to fit in feed tube.	Place in feed tube; shred. Yield: about 4 cups lightly packed.
Leeks 1 pound (2 medium-size)	Sliced	Trim root ends and all but 2 inches of dark green tops. Split lengthwise; rinse and dry. Cut into lengths to fit vertically in feed tube.	Pack vertically in feed tube; slice. Yield: about 4½ cups.
Lettuce, iceberg 1 pound (1 small head)	Shredded	Prepare as directed for Cabbage, shredded.	Process as directed for Cabbage, shredded. Yield: about 5 cups lightly packed.
Mushrooms 1 pound	Sliced	Trim stem bases. Remove a thin slice from one side of enough mushrooms to cover slicing disc at bottom of feed tube (one to three mushrooms).	Arrange sliced mushrooms in bottom of feed tube over disc, with cut sides down and stems pointing in. Stack more mushrooms on top, stems in; slice (see photo on page 14). Yield: about 4½ cups.
	Chopped	Trim stem bases.	Place up to ½ pound at a time in work bowl. Chop, using on-off pulses, until as fine as desired. Yield: about 5 cups.
Onions, dry (red, white, or yellow) 1 small	Sliced	Trim ends; peel. If too large to fit through bottom of feed tube, cut in half lengthwise.	Insert whole or halved onion vertically through bottom of feed tube. Place cover over slicing disc; slice. Yield: about 1½ cups.
	Chopped or minced	Trim ends; peel, and cut into quarters (or eighths, if large).	Place in work bowl; chop, using on-off pulses, until as fine as desired (see photo on page 14). Yield: about 1 cup coarsely chopped, about ½ cup minced.
Onions, green 1 bunch (7 to 9 medium-size)	Sliced	Trim root ends; do not trim tops. Rinse and pat dry. (Slicing technique is pictured on page 14).	With tongs, grasp tops of as many onions as can be held firmly at one time. With motor running, insert root ends down into feed tube. Slice until tongs are halfway into feed tube. Stop machine. Reserve remaining tops for other uses, if desired. Repeat. Yield: about 1 cup.

(Continued on page 15)

Processing Techniques **13**

Processor Basics

Use slicing disc to shred cabbage.
Place as large a wedge as will fit
vertically in feed tube; slice. (You
can also use shredding disc, but
cabbage will turn out very fine and
watery.)

**Before slicing (or chopping) green
onions,** be sure they're dry; damp
onions turn mushy when processed.
While slicing disc turns, lower onions with tongs into feed tube until
tongs are halfway down tube.

To slice mushrooms, cut a thin slice
from one side of bottom mushroom
(or 2 or 3 small mushrooms) to make
it lie flat against disc. Place remaining mushrooms in feed tube with
stems pointing in; slice.

To chop an onion, peel and cut in
half lengthwise; then cut each half
into quarters. (Starting with pieces
of even size ensures even results.)
Place pieces in work bowl and
chop, using on-off pulses.

To French-cut green beans, cut into
lengths to fit horizontally in feed
tube. Stack pieces in feed tube and
slice.

To cut zucchini into julienne strips,
slice zucchini; then stack slices in
feed tube, loading tube from underneath (see photo 2, page 38). Make
sure to pack tube snugly. Put cover
on bowl and slice again.

...Vegetables

Food/Amount	Form/Blade	Basic Preparation	Processing Procedure/Yield
Onions, green *1 bunch* (7 to 9 medium-size)	Chopped	Trim root ends and green tops from onions. (Reserve tops for other uses, if desired.) Then cut white part of each onion into 1-inch lengths.	Place in work bowl. Chop, using on-off pulses, until as fine as desired. Yield: about ½ cup.
Parsley (and other leafy herbs) *up to 2 cups lightly packed sprigs or leaves*	Chopped	Rinse well; discard tough stems. Work bowl, blade, and herbs should be as dry as possible.	Place in work bowl; chop, using on-off pulses, until as fine as desired. Yield: ½ cup sprigs or leaves = ¼ cup.
Pepper, green or red bell *1 medium-size*	Sliced	Cut in half lengthwise; remove seeds and stem.	Place one half, stem end down, in feed tube; slice. Repeat. Yield: about 1¼ cups.
	Chopped	Prepare as directed above; cut into 2-inch chunks.	Place in work bowl; chop, using on-off pulses, until as fine as desired. Yield: about 1 cup.
Potatoes, thin-skinned or russet *1 pound* (about 4 small thin-skinned or 2 small russet)	Sliced	Peel if desired. If necessary, trim to fit feed tube. Trim a thin slice off one end of each potato so it will sit flat over slicing disc.	Place in feed tube, one at a time, trimmed end down; slice. Use sliced potatoes immediately or submerge in cold water to prevent browning Yield: about 3 cups.
	Julienne strips	Prepare as directed above. (Technique for cutting julienne strips is pictured on page 14 for zucchini.)	Slice as directed above. Then process as directed for Celery root, julienne strips. Use immediately or submerge in cold water. Yield: about 3 cups.
	Shredded	Prepare as directed above.	Place in feed tube; shred. Use immediately or submerge in cold water. Yield: about 4 cups lightly packed.
Radishes *1 bunch* (about 12)	Sliced	Trim ends.	Pack vertically in feed tube; slice. Yield: about 1¼ cups.
Shallots *¼ pound* (5 medium-size)	Chopped or minced	Trim ends; peel.	Place in work bowl; chop, using on-off pulses, until as fine as desired. Yield: about 1 cup coarsely chopped, about ½ cup minced.
Squash, zucchini *1 pound* (3 medium-size)	Sliced	Trim ends; cut into lengths to fit vertically in feed tube.	Pack vertically in feed tube; slice. Yield: about 5 cups.
	Julienne strips	Trim ends; cut into lengths to fit horizontally in feed tube. (Technique for cutting julienne strips is pictured on page 14.)	Process as directed for Carrots, julienne strips. Yield: about 3½ cups.
	Shredded	Trim ends; cut to fit vertically in feed tube.	Pack vertically in feed tube; shred. Yield: about 4 cups lightly packed.
Tomatoes *1 pound* (about 4 small)	Sliced	Core. Trim a thin slice from end of one tomato so it will sit flat over slicing disc. If too large to fit vertically through bottom of feed tube, cut in half lengthwise.	Insert trimmed tomato (cut end down) through bottom of feed tube. Place cover over slicing disc; pack feed tube with more tomatoes. Slice, using light pressure with pusher. Yield: about 3 cups.
	Chopped	Core; cut into quarters lengthwise (or eighths, if large) and seed.	Place up to ½ pound at a time in work bowl; chop, using on-off pulses, until as fine as desired. Yield: about 2½ cups.
Turnips *1 pound*	Sliced	Trim ends. Peel; trim sides to fit feed tube, if necessary.	Insert one turnip through bottom of feed tube, then place cover over slicing disc. Pack feed tube with more turnips and slice. Yield: about 4 cups.

Appetizers & First Courses

Spinach Dip

A healthy dose of pepper gives this dip its distinctive authority. It's equally good with vegetables, chips, or crackers.

- **2 cloves garlic**
- **⅓ cup green onion pieces (white part only, cut into 1-inch lengths)**
- **½ cup lightly packed parsley sprigs**
- **1 package (10 oz.) frozen chopped spinach, thawed; or about 1 cup very well drained cooked spinach**
- **1 tablespoon lemon juice**
- **1 cup sour cream**
- **1½ teaspoons pepper**
- **Salt**

Insert metal blade. Mince garlic as directed on page 13; leave in work bowl. Add onion pieces and parsley to work bowl and process until chopped, using on-off pulses.

Drain thawed spinach, then squeeze out as much liquid as possible. Add to work bowl with lemon juice, sour cream, and pepper. Process continuously until blended. Season to taste with salt.

Spoon into a serving bowl; then cover and refrigerate for at least 2 hours or until next day. Makes about 2½ cups.

Blue Cheese & Sour Cream Dip

Bold blue cheese makes a perfect dip for raw vegetables—try carrot sticks, cucumber or zucchini spears, bell pepper strips, small inner romaine lettuce leaves, or cherry tomatoes.

    1 clove garlic
    ⅓ cup mayonnaise, purchased or homemade
       (page 33)
    1 cup sour cream
    3 tablespoons lemon juice
    4 ounces blue-veined cheese
    ½ teaspoon salt

Insert metal blade. Mince garlic as directed on page 13; leave in work bowl. Add mayonnaise, sour cream, lemon juice, cheese, and salt; process continuously (stopping to scrape bowl once or twice) until smooth. Cover and refrigerate for at least 2 hours or until next day. Makes 2 cups.

Pinto Bean Dip

Pinto beans simmered in a flavorful brew of beer, broth, and bay are the heart of this dip. Add cheese, tomato, and cilantro—then scoop up with tortilla chips.

    1 medium-size onion
    1 cup dried pinto beans
    1 can (12 oz.) beer
    1 can (14½ oz.) regular-strength beef broth
       (about 1¾ cups)
    1 bay leaf
    ¼ teaspoon liquid hot pepper seasoning
    1 can (4 oz.) diced green chiles, drained well
    ½ teaspoon each oregano leaves and
       ground cumin
       Garlic salt and pepper
    2 ounces sharp Cheddar cheese
    1 small tomato, quartered and seeded
       Chopped fresh cilantro (coriander)
       Tortilla chips

Insert metal blade. Chop onion as directed on page 13; place in a 3 to 4-quart pan. Rinse and sort beans, discarding any debris, and add to pan along with beer, broth, bay leaf, and hot pepper seasoning. Bring to a boil over high heat; then cover, reduce heat, and simmer until beans mash easily (2½ to 3 hours). Place in work bowl and add chiles, oregano, and cumin; process continuously until smooth. Season to taste with garlic salt and pepper. Spoon into a shallow serving bowl, then cover and refrigerate for at least 2 hours or until next day.

Just before serving, insert shredding disc. Shred cheese as directed on page 8 and sprinkle over bean mixture. Change to metal blade. Finely chop tomato as directed on page 15; sprinkle over cheese. Top with cilantro; offer tortilla chips for dipping. Makes 2½ cups.

Black Caviar Pie

Layers of creamy eggs, green onions, and sour cream smooth the salty spike of caviar in this eye-catching hors d'oeuvre.

    1 jar (3 to 4 oz.) black lumpfish or whitefish
       caviar
    8 medium-size green onions (white part only),
       cut in 1-inch pieces
       Mustard eggs (recipe follows)
    1 jar (2 oz.) sliced pimentos, drained well
    6 ounces cream cheese, cut into chunks
    ½ cup sour cream
       Unsalted crackers

Empty caviar into a fine wire strainer. Rinse with cold water; drain well. Cover and refrigerate.

Insert metal blade. Chop onions as directed on page 15 and set aside. Prepare Mustard eggs; spoon onto a large, flat dish, then spread smoothly into a 10-inch circle. Top with onions and pimentos. Cover and refrigerate until firm (1 hour).

Place cream cheese and sour cream in work bowl; process continuously until soft and smooth. Spread carefully over eggs. Cover and refrigerate for at least 1 hour or until next day.

Just before serving, empty caviar onto a double layer of paper towels; carefully blot dry with more paper towels. Spoon caviar into center of pie. Offer with crackers. Makes 12 to 16 servings.

Mustard eggs. Insert metal blade. Place 6 **hard-cooked eggs,** ⅓ cup **butter** or margarine (softened), and 2 teaspoons each **Dijon mustard** and **white wine vinegar** in work bowl. Process continuously (stopping to scrape bowl often) until smooth. Season to taste with **salt.**

Pea Pods with Mustard Eggs

Chilled fresh Chinese pea pods or sugar snap peas are a sweet and crunchy partner for smooth, buttery egg spread.

½ pound Chinese pea pods (also called snow or sugar peas) or sugar snap peas
½ recipe Mustard eggs (page 17)

Break off ends of pea pods, then remove and discard strings. Rinse pea pods well, pat dry, and place in a plastic bag. Refrigerate until chilled and crisp (at least 4 hours or until next day).

Meanwhile, prepare ½ recipe Mustard eggs. If made ahead, cover and refrigerate until next day (bring to room temperature before serving).

Arrange pea pods on a platter and offer Mustard eggs for dipping. Makes about 4 servings.

Smoked Salmon Mousse

Ease of preparation and light, creamy texture distinguish our version of salmon mousse.

3 ounces smoked salmon or lox, cut into chunks
1 egg yolk
1½ tablespoons lemon juice
3 tablespoons salad oil
2 small cucumbers
Red onion slivers
Watercress sprigs
Thin lemon wedges

Insert metal blade. Place salmon, egg yolk, and lemon juice in work bowl; process continuously until puréed. With motor running, pour oil through feed tube in a thin, steady stream; continue processing until smoothly blended. Cover and refrigerate until cold and thick (at least 1 hour or until next day).

Change to slicing disc. Slice cucumbers as directed on page 13. Arrange equal portions of cucumber on 4 salad plates, overlapping slices slightly in an attractive fan pattern. Mound a spoonful of salmon mousse on or near cucumber. Garnish each serving with a few slivers of onion, 2 or 3 watercress sprigs, and a lemon wedge. Makes 4 servings.

Steak Tartare

(Pictured on facing page)

It's hard to imagine a dish better suited to the food processor than steak tartare. What once required laborious chopping and grinding is now achieved with a few strokes of the pulse button. One job, however, remains to be done the old-fashioned way: be sure to trim the beef carefully before processing.

½ cup lightly packed parsley sprigs
½ small onion
2 tablespoons capers, drained well
1½ pounds lean, boneless beef sirloin, trimmed of fat and cut into chunks
1 egg
½ teaspoon salt
2 teaspoons soy sauce
1 tablespoon Worcestershire
1½ tablespoons lemon juice
¼ teaspoon liquid hot pepper seasoning
Coarsely ground pepper
Garnishes: Watercress sprigs, whole chives, slivered red bell pepper, and whole capers
Melba toast or thinly sliced French bread
Egg yolks and onion rings (optional)

Insert metal blade. Mince parsley, then onion, as directed on pages 15 and 13; set aside. Place capers in work bowl. Process, using on-off pulses, until coarsely chopped. Set aside. Following directions on page 10, coarsely grind beef, a portion at a time (or all at once in a large-capacity processor). Leave in work bowl. Add parsley, onion, capers, egg, salt, soy, Worcestershire, lemon juice, and hot pepper seasoning. Process, using on-off pulses, just until ingredients are combined. Season to taste with pepper. If made ahead, cover and refrigerate for up to 1 hour.

To serve as a first course, divide meat mixture into 6 to 8 equal portions; shape into balls. Place each portion on a plate and flatten slightly. Surround with garnishes. Serve with melba toast.

If desired, place an egg yolk and a few onion rings on each plate; as you eat, mix egg yolk with meat.

To serve buffet style, shape meat mixture into a ball, place on a serving plate, and flatten slightly. Surround with garnishes; serve with melba toast. (Omit egg yolks and onion rings.)

Makes 6 to 8 first-course servings or 16 to 18 servings as part of an appetizer buffet.

Steak Tartare

1 Carefully trim all excess fat from beef. For the best texture, use a naturally tender cut, such as sirloin.

2 Cut beef into even chunks, each about 1 inch square. Cutting ingredients into uniform pieces ensures most evenly processed results.

3 Add mixture of chopped capers and minced onion and parsley to ground sirloin in work bowl. The processor not only grinds and chops, but mixes ingredients and seasonings together.

4 Shape ⅙ to ⅛ of the beef mixture into a ball for each first course serving. To serve as part of a buffet, just mound all beef mixture on a platter.

Garlic-Herb Cheesecake

It looks like the cheesecake you'd serve for dessert, but the flavor is unmistakably *garlic*. Serve thin wedges of this rich, savory cake as a first course or as part of an appetizer buffet.

        Whole wheat press-in crust (recipe follows)
    4 large cloves garlic
    1½ pounds cream cheese, cut into chunks
    3 eggs
    ¼ cup lemon juice
    2½ teaspoons fines herbes or ½ teaspoon *each* summer savory, dry basil, thyme leaves, oregano leaves, and marjoram leaves
        Salt
    2 green onions (including tops), thinly sliced

Prepare crust; set aside.

Insert metal blade. Mince garlic as directed on page 13; leave in work bowl. Add cream cheese to work bowl and process continuously (stopping to scrape bowl often) until soft and smooth. With motor running, pour eggs, lemon juice, and fines herbes through feed tube and continue processing until smooth. Season to taste with salt. Spoon mixture into baked crust. Bake in a 350° oven until center barely jiggles when pan is gently shaken (about 25 minutes). Place pan on a rack and let cake cool to room temperature. If made ahead, cover and refrigerate until next day; serve at room temperature.

To serve, remove pan sides and sprinkle cheesecake with onions. Cut into thin wedges. Makes 16 to 20 servings.

Whole wheat press-in crust. Prepare **Press-in pastry** as directed on page 98, but use 1 cup **whole wheat flour,** 6 tablespoons **butter** or margarine, and 1 **egg.** Omit sugar. Press dough evenly over bottom and about 1¾ inches up sides of a 9-inch spring-form pan or round cake pan with removable bottom. Bake in a 350° oven until lightly browned (about 20 minutes). Use warm or cold.

Cheese Twists

Traditional fare for an English tea, cheese twists also make tempting finger food with cocktails or as part of an appetizer buffet.

    2 ounces Cheddar cheese
    ¾ cup all-purpose flour
    ⅛ teaspoon ground red pepper (cayenne)
    ¼ cup butter or margarine, cut into chunks
    1 egg yolk beaten with 2 tablespoons water

Insert shredding disc. Shred cheese as directed on page 8; leave in work bowl. Change to metal blade and add flour, pepper, and butter to work bowl. Process continuously until mixture resembles fine crumbs. With motor running, pour egg yolk mixture through feed tube and continue processing just until mixture holds together (don't let it form a ball). Gather into a ball with your hands, dust with flour, wrap in plastic wrap, and refrigerate until firm (at least 1 hour or until next day).

On a lightly floured board, roll out dough to a thickness of ¼ inch. With a floured knife, cut into strips ½ inch wide and 3 to 4 inches long. Hold ends of each strip and twist in opposite directions. (If dough becomes soft, refrigerate until easy to handle). Place twists slightly apart on ungreased baking sheets. (At this point, you may freeze twists on baking sheets until firm, then transfer to plastic bags and freeze for up to 1 month.)

Bake in a 400° oven until golden (about 10 minutes; about 14 minutes if frozen). Let cool on racks. Makes about 2 dozen twists.

Almond-Cheddar Ball

Cream cheese and sherry mellow the sharp bite of Cheddar in this festive cheese spread.

    8 ounces sharp Cheddar cheese
    ⅓ cup whole blanched almonds
    4 ounces cream cheese, cut into chunks
    1 tablespoon *each* dry sherry and mayonnaise
    1½ teaspoons Dijon mustard
        Dash of ground red pepper (cayenne)
    3 tablespoons coarsely chopped sweet pickle
        Crackers

Insert shredding disc. Shred Cheddar cheese as directed on page 8; transfer to a mixing bowl. Change to metal blade and coarsely chop almonds as directed on page 12; set aside.

With motor running, drop cream cheese through feed tube and continue processing until smooth. Add sherry, mayonnaise, mustard, pepper, and pickle to work bowl; process continuously (stopping to scrape bowl once or twice) until soft and smooth. Add cream cheese mixture to Cheddar cheese; mix well. Return mixture to work bowl, half at a time (or all at once in a large-capacity processor); process continuously (stopping to scrape bowl once or twice) until blended. Cover and refrigerate until firm.

Shape cheese mixture into a ball, wrap in plastic wrap, and refrigerate for at least 2 hours or for up to 2 weeks. Meanwhile, spread almonds in a shallow baking pan and toast in a 350° oven until golden (about 8 minutes). Let cool.

To serve, roll chilled cheese ball in almonds to coat; let stand at room temperature for 1½ to 2 hours. Serve with crackers. Makes about 3 cups.

Ham & Cheese Triangles

Fragile and translucent from the package, fila dough bakes up crisp and buttery. The flaky pastry lends itself to a variety of fillings; here we offer a favorite flavor combination of ham and Swiss cheese.

 1 **pound cooked ham, trimmed of fat and cut into chunks**
 8 **ounces Swiss cheese**
 7 **green onions**
 3 **eggs**
 2 **tablespoons Dijon mustard**
 ¼ **teaspoon pepper**
 24 **sheets fila (if frozen, thaw according to package directions before using)**
    About ½ cup (¼ lb.) butter or margarine, melted

Insert metal blade. Chop ham as directed on page 10; transfer to a mixing bowl. Change to shredding disc and shred cheese as directed on page 8; add to ham. Change to slicing disc and slice onions as directed on page 13; add to ham mixture. Change to metal blade. Place eggs, mustard, and pepper in work bowl. Process, using on-off pulses, just until combined. Add to ham mixture and stir well.

Unfold fila; cover with plastic wrap to prevent drying. Lay one sheet of fila out flat. Brush lightly with butter (streak in a few places—don't coat whole sheet). Lay another sheet of fila on top, brush again, and top with one more sheet.

Cut stacked fila into eight 2 by 12-inch strips. Place 1 level tablespoon of filling about ½ inch up and in from lower left corner of each strip. Lift right corner and fold diagonally over filling;

folded portion of strip should be a neat triangle. Continue folding strip like a flag to make a triangular pastry. Place pastries on an ungreased rimmed baking sheet; brush tops with butter. Cover with plastic wrap. Repeat stacking, filling, and folding with remaining fila sheets.

Bake in a 400° oven until golden (about 18 minutes). Serve hot. Makes about 5 dozen pastries.

Pear & Parmesan Croustade

For a satisfying and informal first course, offer chilled white wine and slices of this *croustade*—an unusual combination of sweet, tangy, and savory toppings on a crusty baguette base.

 10 **ounces Parmesan cheese**
    Parsley spread (recipe follows)
 1 **slender baguette (18 to 20 inches long)**
 3 **large ripe pears (about 1¾ lbs.** *total***)**
 ¼ **cup lemon juice**
 1 **teaspoon coarsely ground pepper**

Insert metal blade. Grate cheese as directed on page 8; leave 1 cup in work bowl for parsley spread and set remainder aside. Prepare parsley spread; set aside.

Cut baguette in half lengthwise. Place, cut side up, on an unrimmed baking sheet. Broil 6 inches below heat until golden (about 3 minutes). If baguette arches in middle, turn it crust side up and broil until it lies flat again (about 3 minutes). Remove from oven.

Peel and core each pear, then cut each lengthwise (by hand) into 12 to 16 slices. Place in a bowl with lemon juice and mix gently, coating pears to prevent darkening.

Cover baguette halves with parsley spread. Drain pears and arrange diagonally across baguette halves. Sprinkle with reserved cheese, then pepper. Broil 8 inches below heat until cheese begins to melt (about 4 minutes). Cut each half diagonally into pieces and serve on individual plates; eat out of hand. Makes 10 servings.

Parsley spread. Insert metal blade. Add 1½ cups firmly packed **parsley sprigs** and ½ cup **olive oil** to the 1 cup **Parmesan cheese** in work bowl; process continuously until parsley is finely chopped. If made ahead, cover and refrigerate until next day.

Pork Sui Mai

1 Add green onions, water chestnuts, bamboo shoots, and cilantro to minced ginger in work bowl. The processor chops them all at once.

2 Minced vegetables and seasonings flavor freshly ground pork. The finished filling is shaped into walnut-size balls (about 1 tablespoon each) for final assembly.

3 Cut each dough log into twelve 1-inch lengths; then cut each length in half to make a total of 48 pieces. Work with one piece of dough at a time; keep remaining pieces covered.

4 To shape each dumpling, place one portion of filling on dough circle. Bring dough up around filling; pinch in several places to make pleats.

Pork Sui Mai

(Pictured on facing page)

In China, these steamed dumplings are served as *dim sum*, a traditional Cantonese teahouse meal of small savory pastries. For Western diners, they're perfect one-bite hors d'oeuvres. The entrée-size variation makes an interesting addition to a Chinese meal.

> Dumpling dough (recipe follows) or 48 won ton skins
>
> 4 medium-size Oriental dried mushrooms or 4 fresh regular mushroom caps
>
> 1 pound lean, boneless pork butt, trimmed of fat and cut into chunks
>
> 1 quarter-size slice fresh ginger
>
> 2 medium-size green onions (white part only), cut into 1-inch lengths
>
> 10 canned water chestnuts, drained well
>
> ¼ cup canned sliced bamboo shoots, drained well
>
> 1½ tablespoons fresh cilantro (coriander) leaves
>
> 3 tablespoons soy sauce mixed with 1½ tablespoons cornstarch
>
> 1 egg white
>
> 1 small carrot
>
> Salad oil
>
> Green onion brushes (directions follow)
>
> Soy sauce

Prepare dumpling dough. While dough rests, soak dried mushrooms in warm water to cover until pliable (about 30 minutes). Drain well.

Insert metal blade. Grind pork as directed on page 10; transfer to a mixing bowl.

Finely chop ginger as directed on page 13; leave in work bowl. Add onions, water chestnuts, bamboo shoots, and cilantro. Process, using on-off pulses (stopping to scrape bowl often), until all ingredients are finely chopped (bamboo shoots may remain in larger pieces). Add to pork.

Cut off and discard stems from soaked mushrooms; squeeze caps dry. Place soaked (or fresh) mushroom caps in work bowl; chop as directed on page 13. Add to pork mixture; then add soy mixture and egg white and mix well. Divide mixture into 48 balls, 1 tablespoon each.

Change to shredding disc and shred carrot as directed on page 12. Set aside.

Divide dumpling dough in half; roll each half into a 12-inch log. Cut each log into 1-inch lengths, then cut each length in half to make a total of 48 pieces. Keep pieces covered to prevent drying as you shape dumplings.

To make each dumpling, roll one piece of dough on a lightly floured board to make a 3-inch circle (or cut off corners of a won ton skin to form a circle). Place a pork ball on center of dough; bring sides up around pork, making several small pleats, and give the package a light squeeze in the middle. Tap bottom on a flat surface so dumpling will stand upright. Place ¼ teaspoon of the carrot in center of dumpling. Brush lightly with oil; keep covered until all are shaped.

Place dumplings (without crowding) on a greased rack that fits inside a steamer, wok, or deep pan. Pour boiling water into steamer, leaving 1½ inches between water and rack. Cover and steam until pork filling is no longer pink when slashed (about 20 minutes). Garnish with green onion brushes and serve hot, with soy for dipping. Repeat until all dumplings have been cooked.

If made ahead, cover and refrigerate until next day, or freeze for up to 1 month. (Freeze slightly apart on baking sheets until firm; transfer to plastic bags and return to freezer. Space dumplings apart to thaw—they stick if they touch.) To reheat, steam for 5 minutes. Makes 4 dozen dumplings.

Dumpling dough. Insert metal blade. Place 1 cup **all-purpose flour** in work bowl. With motor running, pour ⅓ cup **boiling water** through feed tube; continue processing until dough forms a ball and feels smooth and velvety (about 15 seconds). Remove from work bowl, cover, and let rest at room temperature for 30 minutes.

Green onion brushes. Cut the white part of **green onions** into 1½ to 2-inch lengths. Using scissors or a sharp knife, slash one or both ends of onion pieces lengthwise 3 or 4 times, ½ inch into onion (or 1 inch into onion if only slashing one end). Cover with **ice water.** Refrigerate until ends curl.

Entrée-size Sui Mai

Prepare dough (don't substitute won ton skins) and pork filling as directed for **Pork Sui Mai,** but leave dough in twenty-four 1-inch pieces. Divide filling into 24 balls, about 2 tablespoons each. Roll each piece of dough to a 4½-inch circle; fill and shape as directed for **Pork Sui Mai.** Place ½ teaspoon shredded carrot on each dumpling. Increase steaming time to 30 minutes. Makes 2 dozen dumplings.

Potato Pancakes with Apples & Chèvre

Though the combination sounds un-likely, crisp, buttery potato pancakes, tangy chèvre, and sweet apples complement each other beautifully. The dish works equally well as a first course or a lunch entrée. As a bonus, the pancakes can be cooked hours ahead and re-heated just before serving.

- **4 green onions**
- **1 pound russet potatoes**
- **¼ cup all-purpose flour**
- **2 eggs**
- **2 tablespoons milk or water**
  Salt and pepper
- **½ to ¾ cup (¼ to ⅜ lb.) butter or margarine**
- **1 medium-size red apple**
- **½ cup large walnut pieces (optional)**
- **4 ounces chèvre (goat cheese), such as Montrachet or bûcheron, cut into 6 to 8 rounds or wedges**
  Whole chives or parsley sprigs

Insert slicing disc. Slice onions as directed on page 13; set aside. Change to shredding disc. Peel and shred potatoes as directed on page 15. Immerse shredded potatoes in cold water im-mediately to prevent discoloration.

In a mixing bowl, beat together onions, flour, eggs, and milk. Drain potatoes, squeeze out ex-cess water, and stir into egg mixture. Season to taste with salt and pepper.

Melt 2 tablespoons of the butter in a wide frying pan over medium heat. For each pancake, spoon 1½ tablespoons potato mixture into pan and spread to make a 4-inch-long oval (you can cook 3 or 4 pancakes at a time). Cook, turning once, until golden (3 to 4 minutes per side); add more butter as needed. Place cooked pancakes in a single layer on two 10 by 15-inch rimmed bak-ing sheets. Let cool, then cover and let stand at room temperature while you prepare apple (or for up to 6 hours).

Change to slicing disc; slice apple as directed on page 8. Melt 2 more tablespoons butter in a wide frying pan over medium heat. Add apple slices and cook, uncovered, until slightly translu-cent (about 2 minutes per side); set aside. Add walnuts (if used) to pan and cook, stirring, until lightly toasted (about 3 minutes—be careful not to scorch nuts). At this point, you may cover apple

and walnuts and let stand at room temperature for up to 6 hours.

To serve, bake pancakes, uncovered, in a 400° oven until crisp (8 to 10 minutes). Then stack pancakes on one baking sheet, making 6 to 8 stacks of 3 or 4 cakes each (slightly overlap cakes in each stack). Top each stack with equal portions of apple, cheese, and walnuts (if used); return to oven just until apple and cheese are warm (about 2 minutes). Transfer stacks to individual plates; garnish with chives. Makes 6 to 8 servings.

Molded Chicken Liver Pâté

A layer of gleaming aspic tops this buttery pâté. Its creamy, spreadable texture is achieved quickly and easily with the aid of a food proces-sor. For a simpler, even quicker version, just spoon the mixture into a crock (omit the gelatin and consommé).

- **¼ teaspoon unflavored gelatin**
- **¼ cup water**
- **¼ cup condensed consommé**
- **1 large shallot or 3 green onions (white part only), cut into 1-inch pieces**
- **¾ pound chicken livers**
- **1 teaspoon dry mustard**
- **¼ teaspoon *each* salt, ground nutmeg, and anchovy paste**
  Dash *each* of ground cloves and ground red pepper (cayenne)
- **¾ cup (¼ lb. plus ¼ cup) butter or margarine, cut into chunks**
  Watercress sprigs
  Crackers or cocktail rye bread

Sprinkle gelatin over water in a small pan; let stand for about 5 minutes to soften. Add consom-mé, then place pan over medium heat; stir con-stantly until gelatin is completely dissolved. Pour into a 2½ to 3-cup mold; refrigerate until gelatin is firm.

Insert metal blade. Finely chop shallot as directed on page 15; set aside. Place livers in a 2 to 3-quart pan and add enough water to cover. Bring to a boil over high heat; then cover, reduce heat, and simmer until livers are very tender when pierced (about 20 minutes).

Drain and place in work bowl with mustard, salt, nutmeg, anchovy paste, cloves, and pepper. With motor running, drop butter through feed tube; continue processing until butter is combined and mixture is smooth. Stir in shallot with a spoon. Spread pate over gelatin in mold; cover and refrigerate until firm (at least 6 hours or until next day).

To unmold pâté, dip mold up to rim in hot water for about 5 seconds; tap edge of mold sharply to free pâté. Place a serving plate over mold and, holding plate in place, invert both. Lift off mold; garnish pâté with watercress. Serve with crackers. Makes about 2½ cups.

Sausage-stuffed Mushrooms

Warm, spicy, and oozing with melted cheese, stuffed mushroom caps are a classic appetizer. The processor cuts preparation time to a minimum, and—an extra boon to the busy cook—the savory nibbles can be prepared a day ahead.

- 2 cloves garlic
- 24 to 30 medium-sized mushrooms (*each* about 2 inches in diameter)
- 7 medium-size green onions
- ¾ pound mild Italian sausages, purchased or homemade (page 63), casings removed
- 1 teaspoon Italian herb seasoning or ¼ teaspoon *each* dry basil, dry rosemary, oregano leaves, and thyme leaves
- 1½ teaspoons Worcestershire
- 4 ounces jack cheese
  Olive oil or salad oil

Insert metal blade. Mince garlic as directed on page 13; leave in work bowl. Twist stems off mushrooms. Add stems to work bowl and process, using on-off pulses, until coarsely chopped; leave in work bowl.

Change to slicing disc. Slice onions as directed on page 13. Crumble sausage into a wide frying pan over medium heat. Cook, stirring occasionally, until browned; spoon off and discard excess fat. Add onion mixture, herb seasoning, and Worcestershire. Cook until liquid has evaporated; remove from heat.

Change to shredding disc. Shred cheese as directed on page 8. Stir half the cheese into sausage mixture; set remainder aside.

Generously brush mushroom caps with oil, then spoon about 1 rounded tablespoon filling into each cap. Place caps, filled side up, in a shallow baking pan. Sprinkle with remaining cheese. (At this point, you may cover and refrigerate until next day.) Bake, uncovered, in a 400° oven until filling is hot throughout (about 15 minutes; about 20 minutes if refrigerated). Makes 2 to 2½ dozen appetizers.

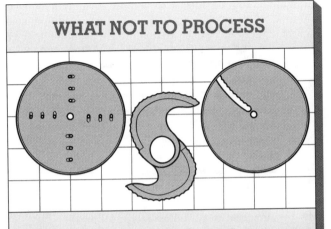

WHAT NOT TO PROCESS

Though the food processor handles an impressive range of foods with ease, it does have a few limitations.

Some foods may actually harm the machine, breaking a blade or even burning out the motor. Before you use your machine, read the manufacturer's guidelines; they'll tell you the foods it won't handle. In general, avoid processing coffee beans, hard grains (such as wheat berries), whole spices, ice, and very sticky candies such as gumdrops. Be sure hard cheeses or frozen meats pass the knife test before processing.

Other foods aren't recommended because they don't process effectively. Some foods crumble apart when sliced in the processor—cauliflower and broccoli flowerets and hard-cooked eggs, for example. (Sliced luncheon meats may also break apart, depending on the brand of food processor; check the manufacturer's instructions.) Slice these foods with a knife. Likewise, soft cheeses such as Brie and Camembert, fruits such as avocados, kiwis, and fully ripe bananas, and most berries are best sliced or chopped with a knife. The processor slices such soft foods unevenly, and tends to purée them instead of chopping.

Finally, we don't recommend mashing cooked potatoes in the processor: the whirling motion of the metal blade brings out the potato starch, resulting in a gluey product.

Vegetable Terrine

(Pictured on facing page)

🍃🍃 Layers of brightly colored vegetables create a striking terrine, a light, fresh alternative to its meat-based namesakes.

- 1 **small onion**
- 3 **medium-size carrots (about 1 lb. *total*)**
- 3 **tablespoons butter or margarine**
- 1 **teaspoon dry tarragon**
- ¼ **cup regular-strength chicken broth or water**
- 10 **tablespoons all-purpose flour**
- 7 **eggs**
  Salt and pepper
  About 1½ pounds spinach, rinsed well, tough stems removed
- ½ **teaspoon grated lemon peel**
- ¼ **teaspoon ground nutmeg**
  Tarragon mayonnaise (recipe follows)

Insert metal blade. Chop onion as directed on page 13; set aside. Change to slicing disc and slice carrots as directed on page 12. Melt butter in a 4 to 5-quart kettle over medium heat. Add onion and cook, stirring, until soft. Stir in carrots, tarragon, and broth. Cover and cook until carrots are very tender to bite (5 to 10 minutes).

Change to metal blade. Place carrot mixture in work bowl; add 6 tablespoons of the flour. With motor running, pour 3 of the eggs through feed tube and continue processing until puréed. Season to taste with salt and pepper; set aside.

Place spinach (with the water that clings to leaves) in kettle used for cooking carrots. Cover and cook over medium heat, stirring once or twice, just until wilted (3 to 5 minutes). Pour into a colander and let cool, then press to extract excess liquid. Place in work bowl with lemon peel, nutmeg, and remaining 4 tablespoons flour. With motor running, pour remaining 4 eggs through feed tube and continue processing until puréed. Season to taste with salt and pepper.

Grease a 6 to 7-cup terrine or straight-sided loaf pan; line with foil. Grease foil. Carefully spoon half the carrot purée into prepared pan, making an even layer. Add all the spinach purée, spooning carefully to keep layers distinct. Top with remaining carrot purée. Smooth top with the back of a spoon. Cover pan tightly with foil.

Set terrine in a larger pan; pour in boiling water to about half the depth of terrine. Bake in a 400° oven until center feels firm when gently pressed (about 1¼ hours). Lift from water bath, uncover, and let cool. If made ahead, cover and refrigerate until next day; serve terrine at room temperature.

To serve, invert a serving plate or board over terrine; holding plate in place, invert both. Lift off terrine and peel off foil. Cut into slices; pass mayonnaise separately. Makes 8 to 10 servings.

Tarragon mayonnaise. In a small bowl, stir together 1 cup **mayonnaise,** purchased or homemade (page 33), and 2 teaspoons chopped **fresh tarragon** (or 1 teaspoon dry tarragon).

Fish Terrine

🍃 Strips of fresh salmon are sandwiched between layers of ground fish and shrimp for a stylish beginning to a special meal.

- ½ **pound medium-size (30 to 40 per lb.) raw shrimp, shelled and deveined**
- ½ **pound non-oily, boneless, white-fleshed fish (such as sole, Greenland turbot, or halibut) cut into pieces**
- 1 **egg**
- ⅓ **cup whipping cream**
- ½ **pound salmon fillet, skinned and boned**
  About 1½ cups Hollandaise Sauce (page 67)
  Butter lettuce leaves

Insert metal blade. Place shrimp and white fish in work bowl; process continuously until coarsely ground. With motor running, pour egg and cream through feed tube and continue processing until smooth. Spread half the fish purée in a greased 1½-quart terrine or straight-sided loaf pan. Cut salmon fillet lengthwise into 1-inch-wide strips; arrange evenly down center of terrine. Top with remaining fish purée. Cover pan with foil and place in a larger pan; pour in boiling water to about half the depth of terrine.

Bake in a 350° oven until center feels firm when lightly touched (40 to 50 minutes). Lift terrine from water bath, uncover, and let cool. When cool, cover and refrigerate for at least 6 hours or until next day.

Just before serving, prepare sauce. Arrange lettuce leaves on individual plates. Cut terrine into thick slices, lift out, and place on lettuce. Spoon 2 to 3 tablespoons sauce beside each portion. Makes 8 to 10 servings.

Vegetable Terrine

1 Pack carrots vertically in feed tube. Alternating thick and thin ends produces the most even slices.

2 Cook onion in butter; then simmer onion and carrots briefly in broth. To achieve a smooth-textured purée, it's important to cook the vegetables until they're very tender.

3 Cooked carrot mixture is puréed with flour and eggs—to add body, and to help purée set as it bakes. Spinach is cooked and puréed next; no need to wash pan or work bowl in between.

4 Spoon spinach purée over first layer of carrot purée; then spoon on remaining carrot purée. Careful layering ensures even bands of color.

Salads & Vegetables

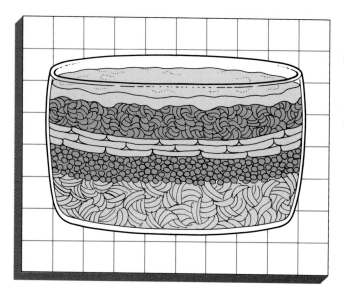

Fresh Yam & Ginger Salad

Crunchy jicama, fresh pineapple, and shreds of sweet, moist yams are combined with a ginger-honey dressing in this colorful salad.

- 3 **quarts water**
- ½ **pound yams (peeled) or carrots**
- 2 **tablespoons lemon juice**
  About ½ pound jicama
- 1 **pineapple (about 3 lbs.)**
- 1 **quarter-size slice fresh ginger**
- 2 **tablespoons salad oil**
- 2 **teaspoons honey**
- 1 **teaspoon grated lemon peel**
  Red leaf lettuce leaves

Bring water to a boil in a 4 to 5-quart kettle over high heat. Meanwhile, insert shredding disc and shred yams as directed for potatoes on page 15. Add yams to boiling water; boil for 30 seconds, then drain well. Mix with lemon juice and set aside. Shred jicama as directed on page 13; set aside.

With a knife, cut off pineapple peel. Cut about half the pineapple into 6 crosswise slices; set aside. Change to metal blade. Mince ginger as directed on page 13; leave in work bowl. Then chop remaining pineapple as directed on page 9.

Pour pineapple mixture into a wire strainer and let drain; reserve juice for other uses.

Squeeze excess liquid from jicama. Place in a bowl and stir in yams, pineapple mixture, oil, honey, and lemon peel. (At this point, you may cover pineapple slices and salad separately and let stand for up to 4 hours.)

Line a platter with lettuce leaves. Arrange pineapple slices on lettuce; top each slice with an equal portion of yam mixture. Makes 6 servings.

Celery Root with Green Beans

Ɛ Ɔ Celery root (sometimes called celeriac or celery knob) is one of the gems of the winter vegetable harvest. Its tough exterior conceals a creamy white interior with a celery-like flavor.

Anchovy dressing (recipe follows)
- ¼ **cup lemon juice**
- 1½ **cups water**
- 1 **celery root (1 to 1½ lbs.), scrubbed**
- ¼ **pound green beans, ends removed**
- 12 **thin slices salami (optional)**

Prepare anchovy dressing; set aside.

Pour lemon juice and 1 cup of the water into a 3 to 4-quart pan. Insert slicing disc. Cut celery root into julienne strips as directed on page 13; immediately drop cut root into lemon water. Bring to a boil over high heat; then cover, reduce heat, and simmer until celery root is tender-crisp to bite (4 to 5 minutes). Drain well, then toss with anchovy dressing.

French-cut beans as directed on page 12. Pour remaining ½ cup water into a 1 to 2-quart pan; bring to a boil over high heat. Add beans, cover, reduce heat, and boil gently until tender to bite (3 to 4 minutes). Drain and plunge into cold water; when cool, drain well. (At this point, you may cover and refrigerate celery root mixture and beans separately for up to 6 hours.)

To serve, toss celery root mixture with beans; mound on a shallow serving dish or on 4 individual plates. Garnish with salami, if desired. Makes 4 servings.

Anchovy dressing. Insert metal blade. With motor running, drop 4 or 5 **anchovy fillets** through feed tube; continue processing until chopped. Add ¼ cup **salad oil,** 2 tablespoons **lemon juice,** ¾ teaspoon **thyme leaves,** and ⅛ teaspoon **pepper;** process until combined.

Jicama Tabbouleh

Ɛ ⊙ Tabbouleh is a Middle Eastern classic, a cooling mixture of bulgur, vegetables, and mint. Jicama gives our version extra crunch.

- 1 **cup bulgur**
- 2 **cups boiling water**
- 2 **teaspoons beef bouillon granules**
- ⅔ **cup each lightly packed fresh mint leaves and parsley sprigs**
- 1 **small stalk celery**
- 1 **small red onion**
  About 1 pound jicama
- 2 **large carrots**
  Garlic dressing (recipe follows)
  Salt
  Inner romaine lettuce leaves
  Fresh mint sprigs

In a large bowl, stir together bulgur, boiling water, and bouillon granules; let stand until water is absorbed (about 1 hour). Pour into a fine wire strainer and let drain.

Insert metal blade. Chop the ⅔ cup mint leaves and parsley as directed on page 15; set aside. Following directions on pages 12 and 13, chop celery, then onion; set aside.

Change to shredding disc. Following directions on pages 13 and 12, shred jicama and set aside; then shred carrots.

Prepare garlic dressing and pour into a large salad bowl. Stir in carrots, jicama, onion, celery, parsley, chopped mint, and drained bulgur; season to taste with salt. If made ahead, cover and refrigerate for up to 4 hours.

Mound tabbouleh on a platter; surround with lettuce leaves and mint sprigs. Offer as an appetizer, to spoon into lettuce leaves and eat out of hand. Or eat alongside lettuce as a salad. Makes about 10 servings.

Garlic dressing. Insert metal blade. Mince 1 large clove **garlic** as directed on page 13; leave in work bowl. Add ⅓ cup **white wine vinegar** to work bowl. With motor running, pour ⅔ cup **salad oil** through feed tube; continue processing until combined.

Avocados with Fresh Salsa

1 Fresh chiles make salsa hot. For a milder salsa, use just one chile, and remove seeds and white pith with a sharp paring knife.

2 Drop chiles through feed tube while motor is running. Be careful when removing cover— fumes are potent! After handling chiles, wash hands; keep them away from face and eyes.

3 To pit an avocado, hold half in one hand and push a knife firmly into pit. Twist knife and pull up—pit lifts out.

4 Drizzle avocados with lemon juice to prevent darkening, then fill natural "nest" in each half with salsa.

Avocados with Fresh Salsa

(Pictured on facing page)

🥄 ◒ Avocado halves make neat nests for a spunky tomato salsa. The pretty red and green "boats" are ideal for a buffet supper.

- **2 tablespoons fresh cilantro (coriander) leaves**
- **1 or 2 small fresh hot green chiles, such as serrano or jalapeño, stemmed (and seeded, if desired)**
- **2 medium-size tomatoes, peeled, quartered, and seeded**
- **6 green onions**
- **2 tablespoons *each* salad oil and red wine vinegar**
- **3 medium-size ripe avocados**
  Lemon juice

Insert metal blade. Chop cilantro as directed for parsley on page 15; leave in work bowl. With motor running, drop chiles through feed tube; continue processing until finely chopped. Transfer chiles and cilantro to a mixing bowl. Chop tomatoes as directed on page 15. Add to chile mixture.

Change to slicing disc. Slice onions as directed on page 13. Stir into chile mixture with oil and vinegar.

Halve and pit avocados; peel if desired, then brush with lemon juice. Place avocado halves on a platter; spoon about ⅓ cup of the salsa into each half. Makes 6 servings.

Confetti Coleslaw

◒ 🔆 🥄 Crisp apple bits, cabbage, carrots, and green onion make a crunchy, colorful counterpart for a sweet-tart yogurt dressing.

- **1 small head red or green cabbage (about 1¼ lbs.)**
- **4 green onions**
- **2 large carrots**
- **2 medium-size tart apples (unpeeled)**
- **1 cup plain yogurt**
- **¼ cup mayonnaise, purchased or homemade (page 33)**
- **3 tablespoons white wine vinegar**
- **1 tablespoon sugar**
- **½ teaspoon dry tarragon**
  Salt and pepper

Insert slicing disc. Shred cabbage as directed on page 12; transfer to a large mixing bowl. Slice onions as directed on page 13 and add to cabbage.

Change to shredding disc. Shred carrots as directed on page 12; add to cabbage mixture.

Change to metal blade. Chop apples as directed on page 8; add to cabbage mixture and stir until thoroughly combined. Place yogurt, mayonnaise, vinegar, sugar, and tarragon in work bowl. Process continuously until combined. (At this point, you may cover and refrigerate dressing and cabbage mixture separately until next day.)

To serve, pour dressing over cabbage mixture; toss to combine. Season to taste with salt and pepper. Makes 6 to 8 servings.

Potato-Pepper Salad

🥄 ◒ Perfect for a summer barbecue, this simple salad combines potatoes and strips of red bell pepper in a dill-seasoned vinaigrette. Use thin-skinned potatoes, red or white—they hold their shape better than russets when sliced and tossed in salads.

- **Dill seed dressing (recipe follows)**
- **2 small red bell peppers, seeded**
- **8 green onions**
- **3 pounds small thin-skinned potatoes, cooked and cooled**
  Salt

Prepare dill seed dressing; set aside.

Insert slicing disc. Following directions on pages 15 and 13, slice bell peppers and leave in work bowl; then slice onions. Transfer onions and peppers to a large salad bowl.

Peel potatoes, if desired. Slice as directed on page 15. Add to pepper mixture; pour in dressing and stir gently to mix. Season to taste with salt. Cover and let stand, stirring occasionally, for 2 to 3 hours. Makes 6 to 8 servings.

Dill seed dressing. Insert metal blade. Mince 2 small cloves **garlic** as directed on page 13; leave in work bowl. Add 6 tablespoons **white wine vinegar,** 1½ tablespoons **Dijon mustard,** 1½ teaspoons **dill seeds,** and ½ teaspoon **pepper** to work bowl. With motor running, pour ¾ cup **salad oil** through feed tube; continue processing until combined.

Chef's Salad

⊖ℬ Slivers of ham and cheese make this salad hearty enough for a lunch or supper entrée.

- ¾ **cup Chili-spiced Thousand Island Dressing (facing page)**
- 1 **medium-size head iceberg lettuce**
- ½ **pound boneless cooked ham (square or rectangular piece)**
- 6 **ounces Cheddar cheese**
- 4 **green onions**
- 2 **hard-cooked eggs**
- 1 **basket cherry tomatoes, halved**
- 1 **can (3¼ oz.) pitted ripe olives, drained well**

Prepare dressing; cover and refrigerate.

Insert slicing disc. Shred lettuce as directed for cabbage on page 12; transfer to a large, shallow salad bowl. Cut ham into lengths to fit vertically in feed tube; stack pieces, then tightly pack into tube and slice. Following directions on page 15 for potatoes (julienne strips), cut cheese into julienne strips; set aside. Slice onions as directed on page 13; set aside.

Change to metal blade. Chop eggs as directed on page 8. Arrange eggs, onions, cheese, ham, and tomatoes on top of lettuce in separate wedge-shaped sections; place olives in center.

Present salad at the table; just before serving, add dressing and toss gently. Makes 6 servings.

Wilted Chinese Cabbage

⊖ Ingredients from the Orient distinguish this salad—mild napa cabbage (often called Chinese cabbage), curly noodles, sesame, and soy.

- ¼ **cup sesame seeds**
- 1 **large head napa cabbage (about 3 lbs.)**
- 6 **green onions**
- 1 **package (3 oz.) Oriental noodle soup mix (any flavor)**
- ¼ **cup sugar**
- ½ **cup salad oil**
- 1 **teaspoon sesame oil**
- 6 **tablespoons white wine vinegar**
- 1 **tablespoon soy sauce**
- ½ **teaspoon pepper**
  Cherry tomato halves
  Fresh cilantro (coriander) sprigs

Toast sesame seeds in a small frying pan over medium-high heat, stirring often, until golden (about 2 minutes). Set aside.

Insert slicing disc. Shred cabbage as directed on page 12. Transfer to a large salad bowl. Slice onions as directed on page 13 and add to cabbage. Break uncooked noodles into small pieces and stir into cabbage mixture.

In a bowl, stir together sugar, salad oil, sesame oil, vinegar, soy, and pepper. Pour over cabbage mixture and toss to mix well; then cover and refrigerate until cabbage is wilted and noodles are soft (2 to 4 hours). Stir well; toss with sesame seeds, then garnish with cherry tomato halves and cilantro. Makes 8 to 10 servings.

Red Cabbage & White Sausage Salad

ℬ⊖ Warmed cabbage teamed with a hot sausage dressing makes a satisfying salad that's perfect for a first course or a light entrée. If you wish, you can assemble the salad at the table, using an electric wok or frying pan.

- 1 **clove garlic**
- 8 **green onions**
  About 1½ pounds red cabbage
- 1 **to 1¼ pounds bockwurst or white bratwurst**
- ¼ **cup salad oil**
- 3 **tablespoons white wine vinegar**
- 2 **tablespoons sugar**
- 1½ **teaspoons *each* celery seeds, Dijon mustard, and Worcestershire**
  Salt and pepper

Insert metal blade. Mince garlic as directed on page 13. Leave in work bowl. Change to slicing disc. Slice onions as directed on page 13; leave in work bowl. Shred cabbage as directed on page 12. Set cabbage mixture aside. Slice sausage as directed on page 10.

Heat oil in a wide frying pan or electric wok over medium-high heat. Add sliced sausage and cook, turning frequently, until browned. Add vinegar, sugar, celery seeds, mustard, and Worcestershire. Bring mixture to a boil; add cabbage mixture, then turn off heat.

Using 2 forks or spoons, lift and turn cabbage until coated with dressing. Season to taste with salt and pepper. Makes 4 to 6 servings.

By now, it's no secret that the food processor makes perfect mayonnaise nearly effortlessly, and whips up a stable, well-emulsified vinaigrette just as easily. For thick and thin dressings alike, the processor speeds preparation by mincing herbs and seasonings and blending ingredients in seconds.

Mayonnaise

- 1 whole large egg or 3 egg yolks
- 1 teaspoon Dijon mustard
- 1 tablespoon white wine vinegar or lemon juice
- 1 cup salad oil
  Salt and pepper (optional)

Insert metal or plastic blade. Place egg, mustard, and vinegar in work bowl; process continuously for 3 seconds to blend well (see page 35). With motor running, pour oil through feed tube—a few drops at a time at first, increasing to a slow, steady stream about ¹⁄₁₆ inch wide. As you add oil, mayonnaise will thicken. Taste; if desired, season with a few more drops vinegar or with salt and pepper. Makes 1 cup.

Chili-spiced Thousand Island Dressing. Insert metal or plastic blade. Place 2 cups **Mayonnaise** in work bowl. Add ½ cup **tomato-based chili sauce,** 2 tablespoons **sweet pickle relish** (drained well), 4 teaspoons **lemon juice,** and 1 teaspoon **chili powder.** Process continuously until blended. Makes 2½ cups.

Watercress Mayonnaise. Insert metal blade. Follow directions for **Mayonnaise,** but omit mustard and increase vinegar to 3 tablespoons. Place ¹⁄₃ cup lightly packed **parsley sprigs,** 2 **green onions** (white part only, cut into 1-inch pieces), ½ cup packed **watercress leaves,** and ¼ teaspoon **dry tarragon** in work bowl with egg; process until blended. Makes 1½ cups.

Green Goddess Dressing

- 3 anchovy fillets
- 3 green onions (white part only, cut into 1-inch lengths)
- ½ cup lightly packed parsley sprigs
- ½ teaspoon dry tarragon
- 1 small clove garlic
- 2 tablespoons tarragon vinegar
- 1 cup mayonnaise, purchased or homemade (this page)
- ½ cup sour cream

Insert metal blade. Cut anchovy fillets in half crosswise. Place anchovies, onions, parsley, and tarragon in work bowl. With motor running, drop garlic through feed tube and continue processing until all ingredients are finely chopped. Add vinegar, mayonnaise, and sour cream to work bowl, then process continuously until dressing is well blended. Makes 1½ cups.

Vinaigrette

- 1 small shallot
- 2 tablespoons Dijon mustard
- 6 tablespoons wine vinegar
- 1 cup olive oil or salad oil (or some of each)
  Salt and pepper

Insert metal blade. Finely chop shallot as directed on page 15; set aside. Place mustard and vinegar in work bowl. With motor running, slowly pour oil through feed tube; continue processing until blended. Return shallot to work bowl; process just to combine. Season to taste with salt and pepper. Makes 1½ cups.

Tangy Shredded Parsnips

⊖ ⊙ Here's a refreshing and unusual presentation of an oft-neglected winter vegetable. Tangy, lemon-flavored mayonnaise complements the slight sweetness of shredded raw parsnips.

- 2 medium-size stalks celery
- 2 medium-size parsnips (about ½ lb. *total*), peeled
- ½ cup mayonnaise, purchased or homemade (page 33)
- 1 tablespoon Dijon mustard
- 2 tablespoons lemon juice
- 3 or 4 large butter lettuce leaves
  Coarsely ground pepper

Insert slicing disc. Slice celery as directed on page 12; leave in work bowl. Change to shredding disc and shred parsnips as directed for carrots on page 12. Place mayonnaise, mustard, and lemon juice in a mixing bowl. Add parsnips and celery; mix gently until blended. Cover and refrigerate for at least 1 hour or until next day. To serve, place a lettuce leaf on each of 3 or 4 plates; top each with a small mound of parsnip mixture. Pass pepper at the table. Makes 3 or 4 servings.

Chicken Salad with Mint

𝄢 ⊖ ⊙ Lime and mint add sprightly flavor to a crunchy chicken and vegetable salad from Vietnam.

- ⅔ cup lightly packed fresh mint leaves
- 1 medium-size white onion
- 3 tablespoons *each* sugar and white (distilled) vinegar
- ¼ teaspoon pepper
- 1 clove garlic
- 1 whole chicken breast, cooked, skinned, and boned
- 2 tablespoons *each* lime juice and soy sauce
- ¼ cup salad oil
- 1 small head cabbage (about 1 lb.)
- 2 large carrots
  Shrimp-flavored rice crackers

Insert metal blade. Chop mint as directed for parsley on page 15 and set aside.

Change to slicing disc. Slice onion as directed on page 13; transfer to a bowl and stir in sugar, vinegar, and pepper. Cover and refrigerate for at least 30 minutes or until next day.

Change to metal blade. Mince garlic as directed on page 13; leave in work bowl. Chop chicken as directed on page 10. Stir chicken, garlic, lime juice, soy, and oil into onion mixture.

Change to slicing disc. Shred cabbage as directed on page 12; add to chicken mixture. Change to shredding disc. Shred carrots as directed on page 12; add to chicken mixture and stir well. Spoon salad into a serving dish and sprinkle mint around edge. Accompany with crackers. Makes 4 to 6 servings.

Swiss Layered Salad

(Pictured on facing page)

⊖ ⊙ Layers of crisp lettuce, peas, Swiss cheese, onion, and creamy dressing add up to a good-looking make-ahead salad. The flavors blend as the salad chills in the refrigerator.

- 1 cup mayonnaise, purchased or homemade (page 33)
- 4 teaspoons Dijon mustard
- ½ teaspoon *each* ground nutmeg and salt
- 1 large head iceberg lettuce
- 1 small red onion
- 8 ounces Swiss cheese
- 1 package (10 oz.) frozen peas, thawed
- 2 teaspoons sugar
- 6 strips bacon, crisply cooked and crumbled

In a bowl, stir together mayonnaise, mustard, nutmeg, and salt; set aside.

Insert slicing disc. Shred lettuce as directed for cabbage on page 12; set aside. Slice onion as directed on page 13; set aside separately. Change to shredding disc. Shred cheese as directed on page 8.

Place half the lettuce in a wide salad bowl that holds at least 4 quarts. Top with half the peas, then half the cheese. Spread half the dressing evenly over cheese; cover with half the onion slices and sprinkle evenly with 1 teaspoon of the sugar. Repeat layering with remaining lettuce, peas, cheese, dressing, onion, and sugar. Cover and refrigerate for at least 2 hours or until next day.

Just before serving, sprinkle bacon evenly over top of salad. Lift out each serving with a spoon and fork, digging all the way to the bottom of the bowl. Makes 6 to 8 servings.

Swiss Layered Salad

1 To make all-yolk mayonnaise, start by separating eggs. Whites are cracked into a small bowl; yolks go directly into work bowl.

2 Slowly pour oil through feed tube in a thin, steady stream (about 1/16 inch wide) while egg-vinegar base whirls in work bowl.

3 All-yolk mayonnaise is thicker than whole-egg mayonnaise, with a more golden color. Mixed with Dijon mustard and nutmeg, it makes a rich, flavorful dressing for the salad.

4 When you layer salad ingredients in a clear bowl, colors, shapes, and textures can be seen.

Springtime Vegetable Tray

Sweet carrots and beets, cool cucumbers, and creamy avocados, all dressed with a tarragon-flavored vinaigrette, are arranged in rows for a bright and colorful buffet offering.

> 1 cup salad oil
> ½ cup tarragon vinegar
> 1 tablespoon sugar
> 2 teaspoons chopped fresh tarragon
>   or 1 teaspoon dry tarragon
>   Salt and pepper
> 1 pound small beets
> 1 pound carrots
> 2 medium-size cucumbers
> 2 or 3 large ripe avocados

In a bowl, stir together oil, vinegar, sugar, and tarragon; season to taste with salt and pepper. Set aside.

Cut off and discard beet tops, leaving 1 to 2 inches attached to crown. Scrub beets well, but do not peel. Place beets in a 3-quart pan and cover with water. Bring to a boil over high heat; cover, reduce heat, and boil gently until tender throughout when pierced (20 to 25 minutes). Drain and let cool.

Insert shredding disc. Shred carrots as directed on page 12; transfer to a bowl and toss with 6 tablespoons of the dressing. Prepare and shred beets as directed on page 12. Transfer to a bowl and toss with 6 tablespoons of the dressing. Cover beets and carrots and refrigerate for at least 4 hours or until next day.

To assemble salad, insert slicing disc. Peel cucumbers, then slice as directed on page 13. Pit and peel avocados, then slice with a knife. Arrange avocados, cucumbers, carrots, and beets in separate rows on a large rimmed tray or platter. Stir remaining dressing; drizzle evenly over avocados and cucumbers. Makes 8 servings.

Hashed Brown Zucchini

Shredded zucchini stars in this light and savory variation on hashed brown potatoes. Serve the little green pancakes with sausages for a leisurely weekend breakfast, or as a vegetable dish for supper.

> 1 clove garlic
> 1 pound zucchini
> ½ teaspoon salt
> 2 eggs
> 6 tablespoons grated Parmesan cheese
>   (see page 8)
>   Pepper
> 3 to 4 tablespoons butter or margarine

Insert metal blade. Mince garlic as directed on page 13; set aside. Change to shredding disc. Shred zucchini as directed on page 15; transfer to a bowl, mix in salt, and let stand for 15 minutes. Squeeze to press out excess moisture. Dry bowl. Place garlic, eggs, and cheese in bowl; stir together, then stir in zucchini. Season to taste with pepper.

Melt 2 tablespoons of the butter in a wide frying pan (preferably one with a nonstick finish) over medium heat. Spoon 2 tablespoons of the zucchini mixture into pan; flatten slightly. Repeat to make several more pancakes. Cook, uncovered, turning once, until browned (4 to 5 minutes per side). Lift out with a spatula; keep warm in a 200° oven. Repeat until all batter is used, adding more butter as needed. Makes 4 servings.

Cheese-crusted Potatoes

Crusty brown on top, soft and creamy inside, this is the kind of dish that invites second helpings. For a slightly less rich version, use a mixture of half broth, half whipping cream.

> 3 ounces Swiss cheese
>   About 1¼ pounds russet potatoes
>   Salt and pepper
>   About 1½ cups whipping cream (or ¾ cup
>   cream and ¾ cup regular-strength beef or
>   chicken broth)

Insert shredding disc. Shred cheese as directed on page 8; set aside.

Change to slicing disc. Peel potatoes, then slice as directed on page 15. Spread potato slices evenly in an ungreased shallow 1½-quart casserole. Sprinkle with salt and pepper, then pour in enough cream to barely cover potatoes.

Cover with foil and bake in a 325° oven for 30 minutes; uncover and bake for 30 more minutes. Sprinkle with cheese and continue to bake until potatoes are tender throughout when pierced (about 15 more minutes). Makes 4 servings.

Garden Patch Sauté

◗ ∮ ◉ This colorful fresh vegetable medley inspires innovation—it's just right for a spur-of-the-moment dinner party or a Sunday night attempt at emptying the vegetable bin. Try using summer squash, broccoli, cauliflower, or peas when they're in season. Whatever combination you choose, you'll have a crunchy, flavorful dish to serve alongside grilled meats or poultry.

- 1 **medium-size onion**
- 1 **medium-size carrot**
- 10 **green beans, ends removed**
- 1 **small red or green bell pepper, seeded**
- 8 **medium-size mushrooms**
- 1 **clove garlic**
- 1 **large tomato, cut into eighths and seeded**
- 2 **ounces Cheddar or jack cheese**
- 2 to 4 **tablespoons salad oil**
- ½ to ¾ **cup fresh corn kernels**
- 1 **teaspoon** *each* **chopped fresh basil and oregano, or ½ teaspoon** *each* **dry basil and oregano leaves**
  Salt and pepper

Insert slicing disc. Slice onion as directed on page 13; leave in work bowl. Slice carrot as directed on page 12; set carrot and onion aside. French-cut green beans as directed on page 12; set aside. Following directions on pages 15 and 13, slice bell pepper, then mushrooms, setting each aside separately.

Change to metal blade. Mince garlic as directed on page 13; leave in work bowl. Chop tomato as directed on page 15. Set tomato and garlic aside.

Change to shredding disc. Shred cheese as directed on page 8 and set aside.

Place a wide frying pan (preferably one with a nonstick finish) over medium-high heat. When pan is hot, add 2 tablespoons of the oil. When oil is hot, add carrot and onion. Cook, stirring constantly, for 2 minutes. Add beans and cook, stirring, for 1½ more minutes. Increase heat to high and add 1 to 2 more tablespoons oil, if needed; then add bell pepper and corn. Cook and stir for 1 more minute. Add tomato, garlic, mushrooms, basil, and oregano; cook, stirring, until carrots are tender-crisp to bite (about 2 more minutes). Sprinkle mixture with cheese; remove pan from heat, cover, and let stand until cheese is melted. Season to taste with salt and pepper. Makes about 4 servings.

TIPS FOR SLICING

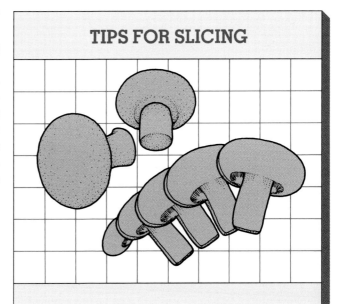

It's easy to produce neat, even slices when you know a few tricks for shopping, preparation, and processing. At the grocery store, keep in mind the size of your machine's feed tube, and learn to select foods which will fit snugly with the least amount of trimming. You'll save time and get neater results. For standard processors, this means choosing a small tomato instead of a large one, a long, narrow potato instead of a round, fat one. Processors with large feed tubes accommodate bigger pieces.

Fresh, top-quality foods slice the most evenly. Produce should be ripe, but still firm and crisp.

Before you process, check the techniques on pages 8 to 15 for basic preparation. For example, rounded vegetables and fruits, such as tomatoes, mushrooms, and limes, cut best if you remove a small slice from one end or side, then set the food flat over the slicing disc. Check to make sure food is at the right temperature, too.

Ready to process? Always have the pusher in place before setting the slicing disc in motion, then use even pressure to push foods toward the disc. In most cases, pressure with the pusher corresponds to the hardness of the food: the softer the food, the lighter the pressure. Be sure to empty the work bowl when food reaches the fill line.

Often, you'll have a piece of food left on top of the slicing disc. Slice it with a knife or reserve for other uses.

Matchstick Zucchini with Marinara Sauce

1 To cut zucchini (or other vegetables) into matchstick pieces, first cut vegetable into lengthwise slices. Remove slices from work bowl before continuing.

2 Stack as many slices as will fit snugly in bottom of feed tube, loading tube from underneath (slice one stack at a time). Carefully place cover on work bowl; slice again.

3 To mince garlic, drop 1 clove at a time through feed tube while metal blade is spinning. Using this method, you can process several cloves in seconds.

4 Cook and stir zucchini quickly in hot olive oil so it stays crisp and crunchy. Serve each portion with bright, fresh-tasting marinara sauce.

Matchstick Zucchini with Marinara Sauce

(Pictured on facing page)

Presentation distinguishes this simple combination. Slender strips of crisp-cooked zucchini are arranged in a mound, then surrounded with a ring of marinara sauce. If you own a French fry disc or one that produces julienne strips, you can use it to cut the zucchini.

- **4 medium-size zucchini (about 1½ lbs. *total*)**
- **2 cloves garlic**
  About 2 cups marinara sauce, purchased or homemade (page 108)
- **2 tablespoons olive oil or salad oil**
  Pepper
  Grated Parmesan cheese (see page 8)

Insert slicing disc. Cut zucchini into julienne strips as shown on facing page. Change to metal blade; mince garlic as directed on page 13. Heat marinara sauce in a small pan over medium heat until hot; keep hot.

Heat oil in a wide frying pan over medium heat. Add zucchini and garlic and cook, lifting and gently stirring, until zucchini is tender-crisp to bite (2 to 3 minutes). Mound zucchini in center of a large platter or 4 salad plates; spoon sauce evenly around (not over) zucchini. Serve immediately. Pass pepper and cheese at the table. Makes 4 servings.

Broccoli with Bacon

This quick and easy broccoli dish pairs well with fish or cheese entrées. The simple bacon and crumb topping perks up cooked cauliflower or spinach, too.

- **4 strips bacon**
- **3 green onions**
  About 1½ pounds broccoli
- **¾ cup fine dry bread crumbs (see page 10)**

Cook bacon in a wide frying pan over medium heat until crisp; lift out, drain, crumble, and set aside. Reserve drippings in pan.

Insert slicing disc. Slice onions as directed on page 13; set aside.

Cut flowerets from broccoli. Trim and discard tough stem ends; peel stems. Cut into lengths to fit vertically in feed tube, then pack into feed tube and slice. Place broccoli on a rack, keeping flowerets and stems separate. Steam, covered, over boiling water until tender to bite (about 3 minutes). Keep warm.

Warm bacon drippings over medium heat. Stir in bread crumbs and onions. Mound broccoli stems in center of a warm platter; surround with flowerets. Evenly sprinkle crumb mixture, then bacon, over stems. Makes about 6 servings.

Fennel with Red Bell Pepper

Though fresh fennel looks much like celery, its flavor is quite different: both the creamy white bulb and the feathery leaves have a cool, faint licorice flavor. Here, sliced fennel and sweet red pepper are cooked briefly in butter, then tossed with a bit of cream.

- **3 or 4 small fennel bulbs (with tops)**
- **1 small onion**
- **1 small red bell pepper, seeded**
- **2 tablespoons butter or margarine**
- **½ cup whipping cream**
  Salt and pepper

Trim fennel stalks just above bulb; reserve leaves and discard stalks. Trim and discard bulb base. Insert metal blade. Place fennel leaves in work bowl and process, using on-off pulses, until chopped; set aside.

Following directions on pages 13 and 15, chop onion, then bell pepper, setting each aside separately. Change to slicing disc. Slice fennel as directed on page 13.

Melt 1 tablespoon of the butter in a wide frying pan over medium-high heat. Add bell pepper and onion and cook, stirring, for 3 minutes. Add remaining 1 tablespoon butter and fennel to pan. Cook, stirring, just until fennel is tender-crisp to bite (about 3 minutes). Transfer fennel mixture to a serving dish. Add cream to pan. Bring to a boil over high heat; then boil, stirring, until reduced by half. Pour over fennel mixture and toss to mix. Season to taste with salt and pepper. Garnish with chopped fennel leaves. Makes about 6 servings.

Spinach-stuffed Tomatoes

◔ Summer's finest red, ripe tomatoes, filled with a savory mixture of fresh spinach and Parmesan, make a perfect warm-weather complement to cold meats. Quick broiling gives them brown, crusty tops.

> 5 ounces Parmesan cheese
> ¾ pound spinach, tough stems removed, rinsed well and patted dry
> 1 medium-size onion
> 8 medium-size firm-ripe tomatoes
> 1 tablespoon butter or margarine
> 1 tablespoon salad oil
> 2 tablespoons fine dry bread crumbs (see page 10)
> ⅛ teaspoon ground nutmeg

Insert metal blade. Grate cheese as directed on page 8; set aside. Place spinach in work bowl, half at a time (or all at once in a large-capacity processor); process, using on-off pulses, until chopped. Set aside. Chop onion as directed on page 13; set aside.

Cut a slice off the top of each tomato, removing about a fourth of tomato. (Reserve slices for other uses, if desired.) With a small spoon, scoop pulp out of tomatoes to make hollow shells. Seed pulp and place in work bowl. Process, using on-off pulses, until chopped. Heat butter and oil in a wide frying pan over medium-high heat. Add onion and cook, stirring, until soft (about 5 minutes). Stir in tomato pulp and spinach and cook, stirring, until spinach is wilted (3 to 4 minutes). Stir in ¾ cup of the cheese, bread crumbs, and nutmeg.

Fill each tomato equally with spinach mixture. Arrange stuffed tomatoes in an ungreased 9-inch square baking pan; sprinkle with remaining cheese. Broil 4 inches below heat just until hot throughout (about 3 minutes). Makes 8 servings.

Squash-Potato Casserole

◔ ⊙ Shreds of butternut squash contribute a slight sweetness to this golden vegetable casserole. It's especially tasty with roast chicken or turkey (you can bake the casserole right alongside the meat).

> ½ cup (¼ lb.) butter or margarine
> 2 eggs
> ½ teaspoon salt
> ¼ teaspoon *each* dry basil and thyme leaves
> ⅛ teaspoon pepper
> 1 clove garlic
> 1 large onion
> About 1 pound butternut squash
> 2 medium-size russet potatoes
> ¼ cup fine dry bread crumbs (see page 10)

Melt 5 tablespoons of the butter in a small pan over medium-low heat; pour into a large mixing bowl. Let cool slightly, then beat in eggs, salt, basil, thyme, and pepper.

Insert metal blade. Mince garlic as directed on page 13; leave in work bowl. Finely chop onion as directed on page 13; add onion and garlic to egg mixture.

Change to shredding disc. Cut squash (if whole) in half lengthwise. Scoop out and discard seeds and fibers. Peel and cut into pieces to fit feed tube; then shred, following directions on page 15 for potatoes. Add to egg mixture. Peel potatoes, then shred as directed on page 15. Add to egg mixture with bread crumbs; stir to blend well. Spread mixture evenly in a greased 10-inch quiche dish or pie pan.

Bake, uncovered, in a 350° oven until lightly browned (about 1 hour). Dot top with remaining 3 tablespoons butter. Makes 6 to 8 servings.

Sautéed Peppers & Pears

⊙ ◔ The combination may sound unlikely, but sweet bell peppers and fall's first fruits make a delicious accompaniment for roast poultry, pork, or ham. Shredded mild cheese melts on top of the hot sauté.

> 3 ounces jack or Münster cheese
> 4 medium-size fresh pimentos or red bell peppers (about 1 lb. *total*), seeded
> 3 medium-size firm-ripe pears or Golden Delicious apples, peeled and cored
> 3 tablespoons butter or margarine

Insert shredding disc. Shred cheese as directed on page 8 and set aside. Change to slicing disc; slice peppers as directed on page 15 and set aside. Slice pears as directed on page 9.

Melt 2 tablespoons of the butter in a 12 to 14-inch frying pan over medium heat. Add peppers and cook, stirring, until peppers begin to soften (about 7 minutes). Then add remaining 1 tablespoon butter and pears. Cook, uncovered, stirring often, until fruit is soft (about 5 more minutes). Pour into a serving dish and immediately sprinkle with cheese. Makes 6 servings.

Meringue-topped Vegetable Custard

What to do with that bumper crop of zucchini? You might try Zucchini Nut Tea Bread (page 87) or Zucchini Custard Torte (page 55)—or this savory casserole, topped with a fluffy cheese-laced meringue that bakes to a beautiful golden brown. It's good as a side dish, but sturdy enough for a supper entrée, too.

1 **large onion**
1 **large green bell pepper, seeded**
5 **or 6 medium-size zucchini (about 2 lbs.** *total*)
2 **tablespoons butter or margarine**
1 **teaspoon** *each* **salt and dry basil**
¼ **teaspoon** *each* **ground nutmeg and pepper**
2 **tablespoons all-purpose flour**
1 **pound Cheddar cheese**
1 **cup sour cream**
6 **eggs, separated**
1½ **tablespoons** *each* **white (distilled) vinegar and water, stirred together**
2 **tablespoons sesame seeds**

Insert metal blade. Chop onion as directed on page 13; set aside. Chop bell pepper as directed on page 15; set aside with onion.

Change to shredding disc. Shred zucchini as directed on page 15. Melt butter in a 12-inch frying pan over medium-high heat. Add zucchini, bell pepper, onion, salt, basil, nutmeg, and pepper. Cook, stirring occasionally, until liquid has evaporated (15 to 20 minutes). Add flour and cook, stirring, for 1 minute; remove from heat and let cool.

Shred cheese as directed on page 8; set aside. In a large mixing bowl, beat together sour cream and egg yolks. Mix in cooled vegetable mixture and 2 cups of the cheese. Spread evenly in a well-greased 1½-quart baking dish.

Wipe work bowl, metal blade, and cover clean with a paper towel. Insert blade; place egg whites in work bowl and process continuously until frothy. With motor running, pour vinegar mixture through feed tube and continue processing until whites hold their shape (see photograph 2, page 102). In a large mixing bowl, fold remaining cheese into egg whites; spread evenly over vegetable mixture. Sprinkle with sesame seeds. Bake in a 350° oven until top is golden brown and a knife inserted in center comes out clean (about 50 minutes). Makes 8 servings.

Duxelles

In French cooking, a dry mushroom mixture called *duxelles* is frequently used to give an intensified mushroom flavor to meat, fish, or poultry. It also makes an elegant addition to stuffings, mushroom sauce, scrambled eggs, omelets, and vegetable dishes. For convenience, you might prepare several batches of duxelles and freeze the mixture in ½-cup portions.

1 **pound mushrooms**
2 **shallots or 2 green onions (white part only, cut into 1-inch lengths)**
¼ **cup butter or margarine**
Salt and pepper

Insert metal blade. Break any large mushrooms into quarters; then place mushrooms in work bowl, half at a time (or all at once in a large-capacity processor). Process, using on-off pulses, until very finely chopped but not puréed. Transfer to a bowl. Finely chop shallots as directed on page 15.

Melt butter in a wide frying pan over medium heat. Add mushrooms and shallots and cook, stirring frequently, until liquid has evaporated and mixture is dark brown (about 15 minutes). Season to taste with salt and pepper. Spoon into small containers, cover, and refrigerate for up to 1 week (freeze for longer storage). Makes about 1 cup.

Duxelles Appetizers

Stir together ¼ cup grated **Parmesan cheese** (see page 8), 2 tablespoons **Duxelles,** and 2 tablespoons **mayonnaise,** purchased or homemade (page 33). Spoon mixture on **melba toast rounds,** using about ½ teaspoon for each. Place on an ungreased baking sheet and broil about 4 inches below heat just until cheese sizzles (2 to 3 minutes).

Soups

California Vichyssoise

🕙 ⊘ Our vichyssoise is a little different from the classic French soup. Though it starts with the traditional leek and potato combination, we've added cucumber for sweetness, and sour cream and yogurt for tang and body. For a lunch or picnic entrée, top each serving with slivers of ham.

1 medium-size onion
4 or 5 medium-size leeks
½ cup (¼ lb.) butter or margarine
1 large cucumber, peeled, seeded, and cut into chunks
4 medium-size thin-skinned potatoes
3 cans (14½ oz. *each*) regular-strength beef broth (about 5½ cups)
1 cup *each* plain yogurt and sour cream
1 pound sliced boiled ham (optional)
  Freshly grated nutmeg
2 or 3 bunches chives, rinsed and snipped

Insert metal blade. Chop onion as directed on page 13; leave in work bowl. Change to slicing disc. Prepare and slice leeks as directed on page 13.

Melt butter in a 5 to 6-quart kettle over medium heat. Add onion and leeks and cook, stirring occasionally, until leeks are very soft and slightly tinged with brown (about 30 minutes).

Change to metal blade. Place cucumber in work bowl and process, using on-off pulses, until chopped. Leave in work bowl. Change to slicing disc. Peel potatoes, then slice as directed on page 15. Add potatoes, cucumber, and half the broth to leek mixture. Bring to a boil over high heat; cover, reduce heat, and simmer until potatoes mash easily (about 30 minutes).

Change to metal blade. Place vegetable mixture, yogurt, and sour cream in work bowl, half or a third at a time, and process continuously until puréed.

Transfer to a large bowl; stir in remaining broth. Cover and refrigerate until cold—at least 3 hours or until next day. (If you plan to transport soup, chill and carry it in a 1-gallon container with a leakproof lid.)

Before serving, cut ham (if used) into julienne strips with a sharp knife. Ladle soup into individual bowls or cups; pass ham, nutmeg, and chives at the table to top individual servings. Makes about 3 quarts (8 to 10 servings).

Garden Gazpacho

⊝ ℬ "A spicy salad in a soup bowl" best describes our gazpacho. Tart, crunchy, and cooling, it combines some of summer's best vegetables—cucumber, tomato, and bell pepper.

- 5 green onions
- 1 clove garlic
- 1 large red or green bell pepper, seeded
- 1 large cucumber, peeled, seeded, and cut into chunks
- 2 large tomatoes, cut into eighths and seeded
- 1 can (2¼ oz.) sliced ripe olives, drained well
- ¼ cup lime juice
- 1 jar (1 qt.) chile-seasoned tomato cocktail
- ½ teaspoon oregano leaves
- ¼ teaspoon ground cumin
  Liquid hot pepper seasoning
  Lime wedges

Insert slicing disc. Slice onions as directed on page 13. Transfer to a large bowl.

Change to metal blade. Mince garlic as directed on page 13; leave in work bowl. Coarsely chop bell pepper as directed on page 15; add pepper and garlic to onions.

Place cucumber in work bowl; process, using on-off pulses, until coarsely chopped. Add to onion mixture. Coarsely chop tomatoes as directed on page 15.

Add tomatoes to onion mixture with olives, lime juice, tomato cocktail, oregano, and cumin. Season to taste with hot pepper seasoning. Cover

and refrigerate until cold (at least 1 hour or until next day). Ladle into small bowls. Pass lime wedges at the table. Makes about 9 cups (6 to 8 servings).

Golden Crookneck Bisque

ℬ Bright yellow summer squash—crookneck or golden zucchini—makes a sunshine-golden bisque with a sweet flavor and a velvety, sippable texture. You'll find golden zucchini at some markets and produce stands; you can also grow it yourself. It has the same cheery color as crookneck squash, but the flavor's slightly mellower.

- 1 medium-size onion
- 2 tablespoons butter or margarine
- 1 medium-size carrot, cut into 1-inch chunks
- 1 pound crookneck squash or golden zucchini, cut into 1-inch chunks
- 1 can (14½ oz.) regular-strength chicken broth (about 1¾ cups)
- ¼ teaspoon each sugar and marjoram leaves
- ¼ cup whipping cream
  Salt and pepper
  Ground nutmeg
  Parsley sprigs

Insert metal blade. Coarsely chop onion as directed on page 13. Melt butter in a 3-quart pan over medium heat; add onion and cook, stirring occasionally, until very soft (about 10 minutes).

Meanwhile, place carrot in work bowl; process, using on-off pulses, until finely chopped. Set aside. Place squash in work bowl, half at a time (or all at once in a large-capacity processor); process, using on-off pulses, until finely chopped. Add squash and carrot to onion and cook, stirring occasionally, for 5 more minutes. Add broth, sugar, and marjoram. Bring to a boil over high heat; then cover, reduce heat, and simmer until carrots are very tender to bite (20 to 25 minutes).

Pour soup into work bowl, half at a time (or all at once in a large-capacity processor); process continuously until puréed. (At this point, you may let purée cool, pack in rigid containers, and freeze for up to 1 month. Thaw before continuing.)

Return purée to pan; stir in cream. Season to taste with salt and pepper. Heat, stirring often, until steaming; then ladle into individual bowls. Sprinkle with nutmeg and garnish with parsley. Makes about 5 cups (about 4 servings).

Sugar Pea Soup

⊖ⴹ This pale green, delicately flavored purée, enriched with whipping cream, is just as delicious chilled as it is hot. For a tangier—and leaner—soup, use plain yogurt in place of the cream.

    8 green onions
    ¼ cup butter or margarine
    1½ pounds Chinese pea pods (also called snow or sugar peas) or sugar snap peas, ends and strings removed
    About 4 cups regular-strength chicken broth
    1 cup whipping cream or plain yogurt
    Salt and pepper
    Plain yogurt or sour cream

Insert slicing disc. Slice onions as directed on page 13. Melt butter in a 4 to 5-quart kettle over medium-high heat; add onions and pea pods and cook, stirring, until pea pods turn bright green (about 5 minutes). Lift out 8 to 16 pea pods and set aside. Add 2 cups of the broth to kettle and bring to a boil; then cover, reduce heat, and simmer until pea pods are very tender to bite (about 20 minutes).

Change to metal blade. Place pea pod mixture in work bowl, half at a time (or all at once in a large-capacity processor), and process continuously until puréed. Firmly press purée through a wire strainer into kettle; discard residue. Stir in cream and 2 more cups broth. Heat, stirring often, until steaming. Add more broth, if necessary, to thin to desired consistency. Season to taste with salt and pepper.

Serve hot or cold. (To serve cold, let cool, then cover and refrigerate for at least 3 hours or until next day.) Ladle soup into bowls; float reserved pea pods and a dollop of yogurt in each bowl. Makes about 10 cups (about 8 servings).

French Onion Soup

⊖ⴹ Cooking the onions very slowly until they take on a rich caramel color is the secret of making good onion soup. For a lighter dish, eliminate the crusty bread and cheese topping and simply garnish the soup with grated Parmesan cheese.

    6 slices French bread, each ½ inch thick
    4 tablespoons butter or margarine
    6 large onions
    1 tablespoon olive oil or salad oil
    1 tablespoon all-purpose flour
    6 cups regular-strength beef broth
    Salt and pepper
    ⅓ cup dry red wine
    4 ounces Swiss cheese

Place bread on a 10 by 15-inch rimmed baking sheet. Bake in a 325° oven until dry (20 to 25 minutes). Spread each slice with 1 teaspoon of the butter; set aside.

Insert slicing disc. Slice onions as directed on page 13. Heat oil and remaining 2 tablespoons butter in a 4-quart pan over medium-low heat. Add onions; cook slowly, uncovered, until soft and caramel colored, but not browned (about 40 minutes). Stir in flour; cook, stirring constantly, until flour is slightly browned (about 2 minutes).

Slowly stir about 1 cup of the broth into onion mixture. Add remaining broth and bring to a boil over medium-high heat, stirring. Cover, reduce heat, and simmer for 30 minutes. Season to taste with salt and pepper; stir in wine. (At this point, you may let cool, then cover and refrigerate until next day. Reheat before continuing.)

Change to shredding disc. Shred cheese as directed on page 8. Ladle hot soup into 6 individual ovenproof soup bowls (1½ to 2-cup size). Top each with a piece of toast, buttered side up; sprinkle with cheese. Bake, uncovered, in a 425° oven for 10 minutes; then broil about 4 inches below heat until cheese is lightly browned. Makes 6 servings.

Creamy Carrot Soup

ⴹ Fresh carrots lend a subtle sweetness to this quick-to-prepare purée, ideal for a first course or a light lunch.

    1 pound carrots, cut into 1-inch chunks
    1 large onion
    2 tablespoons butter or margarine
    2 tablespoons each tomato paste and long-grain rice
    4 cups regular-strength chicken broth
    ½ cup whipping cream
    Salt and pepper
    Parsley sprigs or carrot curls

Insert metal blade. Place carrots in work bowl, half at a time (or all at once in a large-capacity processor); process until finely chopped, using on-off pulses. Set aside. Finely chop onion as directed on page 13.

Melt butter in a 3 to 4-quart pan over medium heat. Add onion and cook, stirring, until soft. Add carrots, tomato paste, rice, and 1½ cups of the broth. Bring to a boil over high heat; then cover, reduce heat, and simmer until carrots are very tender to bite (20 to 25 minutes). Pour soup into work bowl, half at a time (or all at once in a large-capacity processor); process continuously until puréed. (At this point, you may let cool, then cover and refrigerate for up to 2 days.)

Return soup to pan; stir in cream and remaining 2½ cups broth. Bring just to a simmer over medium heat, stirring occasionally. Season to taste with salt and pepper. Ladle into individual bowls; garnish with parsley. Makes about 8 cups (6 to 8 servings).

Leek Soup with Brie

A slice of toast covered with Brie cheese tops each serving of this satisfying soup. The hot, soft cheese adds creaminess and rich, distinctive flavor to chicken broth laden with leeks and mushrooms.

- 6 slices French bread, *each* ½ inch thick
- 4 tablespoons butter or margarine
- 1 clove garlic
- 6 to 9 large leeks
- ½ pound mushrooms
- ½ teaspoon dry tarragon
- ¼ teaspoon white pepper
- 2½ tablespoons all-purpose flour
- 4 cups regular-strength chicken broth
- ⅓ cup whipping cream
- 8 ounces Brie cheese, cut into ½-inch-thick slices

Place bread on a 10 by 15-inch rimmed baking sheet. Bake in a 325° oven until dry (20 to 25 minutes). Spread each slice with 1 teaspoon of the butter; set aside.

Insert metal blade. Mince garlic as directed on page 13; leave in work bowl. Change to slicing disc. Prepare and slice leeks as directed on page 13 (you should have about 8 cups). Set aside. Slice mushrooms as directed on page 13.

Melt remaining 2 tablespoons butter in a 4 to 5-quart kettle over medium heat. Add mushrooms, leeks, garlic, tarragon, and pepper. Cook, stirring, until liquid evaporates and vegetables are very soft (about 15 minutes). Stir in flour. Remove from heat and stir in broth and cream. Return kettle to heat; bring soup to a boil, stirring constantly. (At this point, you may let cool, then cover and refrigerate until next day. Reheat to boiling before continuing.)

Pour soup into 6 ovenproof soup bowls (1½ to 2-cup size). Top each with a piece of toast, buttered side up. Place cheese slices on toast to cover. Bake, uncovered, in a 425° oven until cheese is bubbly (about 10 minutes); then broil about 6 inches below heat until lightly browned (1 to 2 minutes). Makes 6 servings.

Ham & Bean Soup

Smoky ham, tender beans, and a selection of root vegetables mingle in this broth-based soup. Serve it with bread and cheese for a simple wintertime supper.

- 1¼ cups (8 oz.) dried small red beans
- 2 medium-size onions
- 2 tablespoons salad oil
- 1 medium-size turnip, peeled
- 2 large stalks celery
- 8 cups regular-strength chicken or beef broth
- 4 cups water
- 2 pounds ham hocks, cracked and rinsed
  Pepper

Rinse and sort beans, discarding any debris. Set aside.

Insert slicing disc. Slice onions as directed on page 13. Heat oil in a 6 to 8-quart kettle over medium-high heat; add onions and cook, stirring occasionally, until soft (about 10 minutes). Meanwhile, slice turnip as directed on page 15; leave in work bowl. Slice celery as directed on page 12. Add celery, turnip, beans, broth, water, and ham hocks to kettle. Bring to a boil over high heat; cover, reduce heat, and simmer until meat pulls readily from bones (about 4 hours).

Lift out ham hocks. Let cool slightly; pull meat from bones and discard bones, skin, and any fat. Return meat to soup. Skim and discard fat from broth. Season to taste with pepper and serve hot. Makes about 3 quarts (6 to 8 main-dish servings).

TIPS FOR PURÉEING

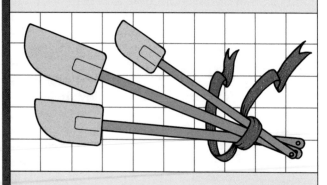

Whether it's for soups, terrines, dips, or baby fare, the processor makes velvety purées in seconds.

To make a purée, start with raw or cooked fruit or fish, cooked poultry or meat, or cooked vegetables (for best results, cook vegetables until very tender). We don't recommend puréeing starchy vegetables such as potatoes or rutabagas if they're to be served mashed. (You can purée these vegetables with liquid for soup.)

Remove and discard any cores, seeds, pits, bones, or gristle from food to be puréed; then cut it into 1 to 2-inch chunks. Next, insert metal blade and add at least ½ cup or up to 2 cups food, plus enough liquid—juice, water, milk, or broth—for even processing. The processor purées thick mixtures more efficiently than thin, watery ones, so keep added liquid to a minimum. Soft, juicy fruits and vegetables, such as berries and tomatoes, need little or no liquid. For firmer foods (carrots and meats, for example), start with 3 tablespoons liquid for each 2 cups food; add more liquid, a tablespoon at a time, if needed, for a smooth purée.

After adding liquid, put cover in place; then process continuously (stopping to scrape bowl once or twice) until smooth. Two cups of solid food yield about 1 cup purée.

Baby food. To make quick, fresh, and inexpensive baby food with your processor, just follow the guidelines above for preparation and puréeing. Try different combinations, such as bananas and peaches or cooked beef and carrots, using ingredients you've prepared for the rest of the family.

Curried Broccoli & Cheddar Soup

All-season vegetables are the backbone of this curry-spiked soup. You simmer potatoes, carrots, and broccoli until soft, then purée half of them to provide a smooth, golden backdrop for tender-crisp broccoli flowerets. Shredded Cheddar cheese is stirred in at the last minute.

About 1½ pounds broccoli
1 **medium-size onion**
¼ **cup butter or margarine**
1 **tablespoon curry powder**
4 **medium-size carrots**
2 **large thin-skinned potatoes**
1 **large can (49½ oz.) regular-strength chicken broth (about 6 cups)**
1 **cup milk**
12 **ounces Cheddar cheese**

Trim flowerets from broccoli and cut into small pieces. Trim and discard tough stem ends, then peel stems. Set broccoli flowerets and stems aside separately.

Insert metal blade. Chop onion as directed on page 13. Melt butter in a 5 to 6-quart kettle over medium heat. Add onion and curry powder and cook, stirring occasionally, until onion is soft (about 5 minutes).

Meanwhile, change to slicing disc. Cut broccoli stems into lengths to fit vertically in feed tube; pack into feed tube and slice. Leave in work bowl. Slice carrots as directed on page 12; add carrots and broccoli to onion mixture. Then slice potatoes as directed on page 15.

Add potatoes and broth to onion mixture. Bring to a boil over high heat; cover, reduce heat, and simmer until potatoes mash easily (about 30 minutes).

Change to metal blade. Using a slotted spoon, transfer about half the vegetables to work bowl and process continuously until puréed. Return purée to kettle.

Bring soup to a boil over high heat; add broccoli flowerets and milk. Reduce heat and simmer, uncovered, just until flowerets are tender to bite.

Meanwhile, change to shredding disc and shred cheese as directed on page 8. Add cheese to soup, a handful at a time, stirring until melted after each addition. Makes about 10 cups (8 to 10 servings).

Bacon Vegetable Soup

🌙 ⟲ Ideal for a soup and sandwich supper, this soup owes its delicate look to pretty julienne strips of carrot and potato—a breeze to prepare in the food processor. A *chiffonade* of romaine lettuce strips garnishes each serving. (For a slightly thicker soup, stir in a mixture of cream and cornstarch.)

- 6 strips bacon, coarsely chopped
- 1 medium-size onion
- ½ pound mushrooms
- 1 large carrot
- 2 medium-size thin-skinned potatoes
- 4 cups regular-strength chicken broth
- 1 bay leaf
- ⅛ to ¼ teaspoon ground red pepper (cayenne)
- ½ cup whipping cream (optional)
- 1 tablespoon cornstarch (optional)
- Pepper
- 5 large outer romaine lettuce leaves

In a 5 to 6-quart kettle over medium-high heat, cook bacon, stirring often, until browned and crisp. Spoon off and discard all but 2 tablespoons drippings.

Insert metal blade. Chop onion as directed on page 13; leave in work bowl. Change to slicing disc and slice mushrooms as directed on page 13. Add vegetables to bacon and cook, stirring often, until onion is soft (about 7 minutes). Remove from heat.

Cut carrot into julienne strips as directed on page 12; set aside. Peel potatoes and cut into julienne strips as directed on page 15; stir into bacon mixture with carrot, broth, and bay leaf. (If you prefer a slightly thicker soup, stir together cream and cornstarch until smooth, then stir into soup.)

Bring to a boil over high heat, stirring constantly. Reduce heat and simmer, uncovered, stirring occasionally, until carrot and potatoes are tender to bite (about 4 minutes). Season to taste with pepper.

Wipe work bowl, cover, and slicing disc dry with a paper towel. Remove cores from romaine leaves. Cut leaves into lengths to fit vertically in feed tube; divide into 2 stacks. Place one stack vertically in feed tube, folding edges in; slice. Repeat with remaining stack. Ladle soup into individual bowls; garnish with romaine strips. Makes about 6½ cups (about 5 servings).

Sweet & Sour Borscht

🌙 ⊙ ⟲ There's nothing more welcome on a chilly night than a steaming bowl of soup. Here's a hearty, warming meal-in-a-bowl that's perfect for such an occasion. Preparation is surprisingly quick, since the processor grinds the meat and chops and shreds all the vegetables for you. Offer thick slices of Dark & Hearty Rye Bread (page 90) or Whole Wheat Country Loaf (page 89) and butter to complete a simple and satisfying wintertime menu.

- 3 medium-size beets with leafy tops
- 1 small onion
- 1 pound lean, boneless pork, trimmed of fat and cut into chunks
- 1 tablespoon salad oil
- 2 large carrots
- ½ small head red or green cabbage
- ¼ cup lemon juice
- 2½ tablespoons sugar
- ¼ teaspoon dill weed
- 4 cups regular-strength chicken broth
- 2 cups water
- Salt and pepper
- Plain yogurt

Insert metal blade. Discard stems and coarse leaves from beets; reserve tender leaves. Rinse and dry reserved leaves, then place in work bowl and process, using on-off pulses, until coarsely chopped. Set aside. Chop onion as directed on page 13; set aside. Grind pork, a portion at a time (or all at once in a large-capacity processor), as directed on page 10.

Heat oil in a 5-quart kettle over medium heat. Add pork and onion; cook, stirring, until meat is browned.

Meanwhile, change to shredding disc. Following directions on page 12, shred carrots; then shred raw beets as directed for cooked beets. Set aside. Change to slicing disc and shred cabbage as directed on page 12.

Add cabbage, carrots, beets and beet leaves, lemon juice, sugar, dill weed, broth, and water to browned meat in kettle. Bring to a boil over high heat; then cover, reduce heat, and simmer until cabbage is tender to bite (about 45 minutes). Season to taste with salt and pepper. Ladle into individual bowls; pass yogurt to spoon into individual portions. Makes about 10 cups (4 to 6 main-dish servings).

Lamb-stuffed Meatball Soup

⑧ This Armenian specialty, called *kufta*, is like a meatball inside a meatball: cooked, seasoned lamb is wrapped in a jacket of uncooked lamb, then poached in broth.

> 1 **cup lightly packed parsley sprigs**
> 1 **small onion**
> ¾ **pound lean ground lamb**
> 2 **tablespoons lemon juice**
> 2 **teaspoons paprika**
> ½ **teaspoon ground red pepper (cayenne)**
>   **Salt and black pepper**
>   **Lamb shells (recipe follows)**
> 8 **cups regular-strength chicken broth**
>   **Parsley sprigs**
>   **Plain yogurt**

Insert metal blade. Following directions on pages 15 and 13, chop the 1 cup parsley and set aside; then chop onion. Finely crumble lamb into a wide frying pan. Add onion and cook over medium-high heat, stirring, for 5 minutes. Add lemon juice, paprika, and red pepper; continue to cook, stirring, until meat is no longer pink (about 10 minutes). Remove from heat; mix in chopped parsley, then season to taste with salt and black pepper. Let cool.

Prepare lamb shells. Moisten hands with water and firmly pat each lamb shell portion into a round patty about 4 inches across. Spoon about 1 tablespoon of the cooked lamb mixture into center of each patty. Bring edges of patty together; pinch to seal. Pat smooth. Set meatballs on a wax-paper-lined baking pan. (At this point, you may cover and refrigerate until next day.)

Pour broth into a 5 to 6-quart kettle and bring to a boil over high heat. Reduce heat to low and add meatballs. (Broth should bubble only occasionally; if cooked rapidly, kufta tend to pop open.) Cover and cook until shells are firm throughout (about 10 minutes, about 15 minutes if refrigerated; cut to test). Skim and discard fat from broth. Ladle meatballs and broth into wide soup bowls and garnish with parsley; pass yogurt at the table. Makes about 3½ quarts (8 main-dish servings).

Lamb shells. Insert metal blade. Place 2¼ pounds **lean ground lamb** and ¾ cup **whole wheat flour** in work bowl, half at a time (or all at once in a large-capacity processor). Process continuously until smoothly blended. Divide into 24 equal pieces.

Mexican Meatball Soup

Combine 1½ pounds **lean ground beef**, ¼ cup **all-purpose flour**, 2 **eggs**, 1 teaspoon **oregano leaves**, and ½ cup **regular-strength chicken broth**. Season to taste with **salt** and **pepper**. Pour 7½ more cups broth into an 8-quart kettle; add 1 large **onion**, chopped (see page 13). Bring to a boil over high heat, then reduce heat to low. Quickly shape beef mixture into 1½-inch balls, dropping them into broth as shaped. Simmer, uncovered, until meatballs are no longer pink when slashed (about 25 minutes). Add ⅓ cup chopped **fresh coriander (cilantro)** (see Parsley, page 15.) Ladle meatballs and broth into soup bowls. Pass **lime wedges** at the table. Makes about 3 quarts (8 main-dish servings).

Minestrone

⑧ Ⓖ A likely candidate for a casual supper party, this hearty minestrone uses a whole garden's worth of fresh vegetables.

>   **Soaked beans (directions follow)**
> 1 **pound mild Italian sausages, purchased or homemade (page 63)**
> 8 **cups water**
> 5 **ounces Parmesan cheese**
> ½ **cup *each* lightly packed celery leaves and parsley sprigs**
> 3 **cloves garlic**
> 1 **large onion**
> 2 **tablespoons olive oil or salad oil**
> ¼ **pound salt pork or *pancetta* (Italian-style bacon), minced**
> 1 **can (14½ oz.) pear-shaped tomatoes**
> 4 **cups regular-strength chicken broth**
> 2 **medium-size carrots**
> 3 **large stalks celery**
> 2 **small thin-skinned potatoes**
> 2 **medium-size zucchini**
> 1 **small head cabbage**
> 1 **cup lightly packed fresh basil leaves (optional)**
>   **Salt and pepper**

Prepare soaked beans and place in a 4 to 5-quart kettle. Pierce sausage casings in several places;

add sausages and water to kettle. Bring to a boil over high heat; then cover, reduce heat, and simmer for 20 minutes; remove sausages and set aside. Continue simmering beans until they mash easily (25 to 50 more minutes).

Insert metal blade. Ladle about half the beans and ½ cup of the cooking liquid into work bowl; process, using on-off pulses, until coarsely puréed. Return puréed beans to cooking liquid; set aside.

Wipe work bowl, blade, and cover dry with a paper towel. Grate cheese as directed on page 8; place in a small serving bowl and set aside.

Place celery leaves and parsley in work bowl; finely chop as directed for parsley on page 15. Set aside. Mince garlic as directed on page 13; leave in work bowl. Chop onion as directed on page 13.

Heat oil in a 6 to 8-quart kettle over medium heat. Add salt pork, onion, garlic, parsley, and celery leaves; cook, stirring often, until onion is soft. Place tomatoes and their liquid in work bowl; process, using on-off pulses, until coarsely chopped. Add tomatoes, broth, beans, and bean cooking liquid to kettle.

Change to slicing disc. Following directions on page 12, slice carrots, then celery; add both to kettle. Peel potatoes; slice as directed on page 15 and add to kettle. Bring to a boil over high heat. Cover, reduce heat, and simmer for 15 minutes.

Following directions on pages 15 and 12, slice zucchini, then shred cabbage; add to kettle. Slice sausages with a knife; add to kettle. Simmer until zucchini is tender to bite (8 to 10 minutes). Stir basil (if used) into soup, then season to taste with salt and pepper. Pass cheese at the table. Makes about 4 quarts (about 8 main-dish servings).

Soaked beans. Rinse and sort 2 cups (12 oz.) dried **Great Northern beans,** discarding any debris. Place in a 3 to 4-quart pan with 6 cups **water.** Bring to a boil over high heat; boil for 2 minutes. Remove from heat; cover and let stand for 1 hour. Drain beans and use.

Cod Chowder

A long-standing American classic, cod chowder starts with a stock made by simmering fish trimmings. Finishing the chowder is fast— you just add fresh vegetables, rice, and chunks of fish to the richly flavored stock.

1 **whole mild-flavored, white-fleshed fish,** such as rock cod, sea bass, or red snapper (3 to 3½ pounds); or 2½ pounds fillets and 1 pound fish trimmings
6 **cups water**
2 **bottles (8 oz.** *each***) clam juice**
1 **bay leaf**
1 **cup lightly packed parsley sprigs**
2 **cloves garlic**
1 **large onion**
½ **cup (¼ lb.) butter or margarine**
2 **large stalks celery**
2 **medium-size carrots**
¼ **cup all-purpose flour**
4 **small thin-skinned potatoes**
¾ **teaspoon thyme leaves**
½ **cup long-grain rice**
Salt and pepper

Fillet fish (or have it done at the fish market), reserving all trimmings. Wrap fish fillets and refrigerate. Place trimmings in an 8-quart kettle; add water, clam juice, and bay leaf. Bring to a boil over high heat; then cover, reduce heat, and simmer for 1 hour. Pour through a wire strainer; discard bones, skin, and bay leaf. Set fish stock aside (you should have about 8 cups). Rinse and dry kettle.

Insert metal blade. Chop parsley as directed on page 15; set aside. Mince garlic as directed on page 13; leave in work bowl. Chop onion as directed on page 13. Melt butter in kettle over medium heat; add onion and garlic and cook, stirring, until onion is soft (about 5 minutes).

Meanwhile, change to slicing disc. Following directions on page 12, slice celery, then carrots; add to onion mixture and cook, stirring occasionally, until onion is very soft (about 5 more minutes). Stir in flour and cook, stirring, for 1 minute. Gradually add fish stock and cook, stirring occasionally, until mixture boils.

Meanwhile, peel potatoes, then slice as directed on page 15. Add to stock with parsley and thyme. Bring to a boil over high heat; stir in rice. Cover, reduce heat, and simmer until potatoes are tender to bite (about 20 minutes).

Change to metal blade. With a slotted spoon, transfer about a third of the vegetables to work bowl; process continuously until smooth. Return to kettle.

Cut fish fillets into 1-inch squares; add to kettle, cover, and continue to simmer, stirring occasionally, until fish is opaque throughout (about 10 minutes—prod with a fork to test). Season to taste with salt and pepper. Makes about 3½ quarts (8 to 10 main-dish servings).

Eggs & Cheese

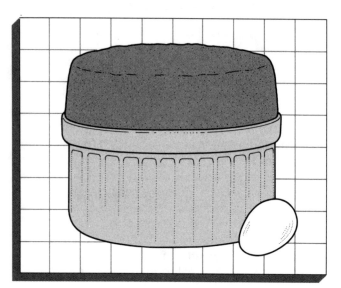

Oriental Omelet

Delicate vegetables cooked in an Oriental-style sauce distinguish this omelet. It's an ideal lunch or supper dish for two.

Cooking sauce (recipe follows)
4 **large mushrooms**
1 **stalk celery**
1 **medium-size carrot**
2 **tablespoons salad oil**
4 **or 5 eggs**
2 **tablespoons water**
  Salt and pepper
2 **tablespoons butter or margarine**

Prepare cooking sauce; set aside.

Insert slicing disc. Following directions on pages 13 and 12, slice mushrooms, then celery; set aside. Cut carrot into julienne strips as directed on page 12. Heat oil in a wide frying pan over medium heat. Add carrot, celery, and mushrooms; cook, stirring, until carrot is tender-crisp to bite (4 to 5 minutes). Add cooking sauce and cook, stirring, until sauce boils. Remove from heat.

In a bowl, lightly beat eggs with water; season to taste with salt and pepper. Melt butter in a wide frying pan over medium-high heat. Add egg mixture and cook until softly set, gently lifting cooked portion to allow uncooked portion to flow underneath. Fold omelet out of pan and cover with vegetable mixture. Makes 2 servings.

Cooking sauce. In a small bowl, combine 1 teaspoon *each* **cornstarch** and **sugar,** 1 tablespoon **dry sherry,** 2 tablespoons **soy sauce,** and ¼ cup **water.** Stir until smoothly blended.

Huevos Rancheros

Eggs cooked in chunky, zesty tomato sauce are a good choice for brunch or supper. You might offer cornsticks or warmed tortillas alongside.

- 2 ounces jack cheese
- 1 clove garlic
- 1 small onion, cut into chunks
- ½ green bell pepper, seeded and cut into chunks
- 2 tablespoons salad oil
- 1 can (about 1 lb.) tomatoes
- ½ teaspoon salt
- ½ to 1 teaspoon chili powder
- 1½ teaspoons all-purpose flour
- 6 eggs

Insert shredding disc. Shred cheese as directed on page 8; set aside.

Change to metal blade. Mince garlic as directed on page 13; leave in work bowl. Add onion and bell pepper to work bowl and process, using on-off pulses, until coarsely chopped.

Heat oil in a wide frying pan over medium-high heat. Add pepper, onion, and garlic. Cook, stirring occasionally, until onion is soft (about 5 minutes). Meanwhile, place tomatoes and their liquid, salt, and chili powder in work bowl. Process, using on-off pulses, until tomatoes are coarsely chopped.

Sprinkle flour over onion mixture and stir in. Add tomatoes. Reduce heat to medium and cook, stirring occasionally, until sauce is thickened— about 4 minutes. (At this point, you may cover and refrigerate until next day. Before adding eggs, reheat sauce over medium heat.)

Make 6 evenly spaced depressions in sauce; carefully break an egg into each. Sprinkle cheese over eggs. Cover pan and cook over low heat until eggs are done to your liking (7 to 10 minutes). Makes 3 to 6 servings.

Cheese Soufflé

A perfect soufflé has always been the mark of a skilled cook, and it's no secret that properly beaten egg whites are the key to success. The processor beats them to perfection in seconds, giving you a finished soufflé that's a light, puffy, golden brown dome.

To vary this classic soufflé, sprinkle the buttered dish with freshly grated Parmesan cheese before adding the egg mixture. Or try using shredded Gruyère or Swiss cheese in place of Cheddar.

   Butter or margarine
- 4 ounces sharp Cheddar cheese
- 3 tablespoons all-purpose flour
- 1 cup milk
   Dash of ground red pepper (cayenne)
- ¼ teaspoon *each* dry mustard and salt
- 4 eggs, separated
- 1 tablespoon *each* white (distilled) vinegar and water, stirred together

Preheat oven to 375°. Butter a 1½-quart soufflé dish, using about 1 teaspoon butter.

Insert shredding disc. Shred cheese as directed on page 8; set aside.

Melt 3 tablespoons butter in a 2 to 3-quart pan over medium heat; stir in flour and cook until bubbly. Combine milk, pepper, mustard, and salt; stir in gradually. Cook, stirring, until sauce boils and thickens. Add cheese and continue to cook and stir until cheese is melted. Remove pan from heat; add egg yolks, stirring constantly until blended. Set aside.

Thoroughly wash and dry work bowl and cover. Insert metal blade. Place egg whites in work bowl and process continuously until frothy. With motor running, pour vinegar mixture through feed tube and continue processing until egg whites hold their shape (see photograph 2, page 102). Thoroughly fold about a third of the beaten whites into sauce mixture; then fold in remaining whites. Pour into prepared dish. With the tip of a knife, draw a circle on the surface about 1 inch in from rim of dish.

For a moist soufflé, bake until top is golden brown and center jiggles slightly when dish is gently shaken (25 to 30 minutes). For a firmer soufflé, bake until center feels firm when lightly touched (30 to 35 minutes). Serve immediately. Makes 4 servings.

Vegetable Frittata Loaf

A frittata is an Italian version of the classic French omelet; instead of folding the omelet around a filling, you cook eggs and filling together. This frittata is tucked inside a loaf of French bread, making a nutritious one-dish meal that's perfect for a picnic.

- 1 **round loaf (1½ lbs.) unsliced French bread, about 12 inches in diameter**
- 5 **tablespoons olive oil**
- 2½ **ounces Parmesan cheese**
- ¾ **pound mild Italian sausages, purchased or homemade (page 63), casings removed**
- 2 **cloves garlic**
- 1 **small onion**
- 1 **large tomato, peeled, cut into eighths, and seeded**
- 2 **small zucchini**
- ½ **cup lightly packed fresh basil leaves or 2 teaspoons dry basil**
- 9 **eggs**
- ½ **teaspoon *each* salt and pepper**

Cut bread in half horizontally. Hollow out halves, leaving a ½-inch-thick shell. Brush 3 tablespoons of the oil over inside. Reassemble loaf, wrap in foil, and warm in a 350° oven for 10 to 15 minutes.

Meanwhile, insert metal blade. Grate cheese as directed on page 8; set aside.

Crumble sausage into a 9 to 10-inch frying pan (preferably one with a nonstick finish). Cook over medium heat, stirring occasionally, until browned. While sausage cooks, mince garlic as directed on page 13; leave in work bowl. Chop onion as directed on page 13; set onion and garlic aside. Chop tomato as directed on page 15; leave in work bowl. Change to slicing disc and slice zucchini as directed on page 15.

Spoon off and discard all but 2 tablespoons drippings from sausage; set meat aside. Add onion and garlic to pan and cook, stirring, until onion is soft. Add zucchini and tomato; cook, stirring, until liquid has evaporated. Remove from heat. Change to metal blade and chop fresh basil as directed for parsley on page 15; add to vegetable mixture.

In a large bowl, beat eggs with salt and pepper. Stir in vegetable mixture and sausage.

Wipe pan clean. Heat 1 tablespoon of the oil over medium heat. Pour in egg mixture. With a wide spatula, push egg toward center as it sets to allow uncooked portion to flow underneath.

Shake pan often to keep frittata free. When frittata is set and browned on the bottom, invert a 12-inch plate over pan; flip frittata onto plate. Return pan to heat and add remaining 1 tablespoon oil; slide frittata back into pan and cook until bottom is lightly browned. Sprinkle with cheese.

Unwrap loaf; place bottom half over frittata. Invert pan so frittata drops into loaf. Set top half of loaf in place. Serve at once, or wrap in foil and keep warm in an insulated chest for up to 4 hours. If made ahead, let cool, then wrap in foil and refrigerate until next day. Reheat, wrapped, in a 300° oven until hot throughout (1 to 1¼ hours). To serve, cut into wedges with a serrated knife and eat out of hand. Makes 7 or 8 servings.

Crustless Cheese & Vegetable Pie

Two kinds of cheese—ricotta and jack—make a mild, creamy base for this vegetable-laden pie. For a satisfying warm-weather supper, accompany wedges of pie with crusty bread and wine.

- ¼ **pound mushrooms**
- 1 **small zucchini**
- 1 **clove garlic**
- ⅓ **cup butter or margarine**
- ¼ **pound cooked ham, trimmed of fat and cut into chunks**
- 4 **eggs**
- 2 **cups ricotta cheese**
- 4 **ounces jack cheese**
- 1 **package (10 oz.) frozen chopped spinach, thawed and squeezed dry**
- ½ **teaspoon dill weed**
- ¼ **teaspoon pepper**

Insert slicing disc. Slice mushrooms, then zucchini as directed on pages 13 and 15; set aside. Change to metal blade and mince garlic as directed on page 13.

Melt butter in a wide frying pan over medium heat. Add garlic, zucchini, and mushrooms; cook, stirring occasionally, just until vegetables are soft (about 3 minutes). Meanwhile, chop ham as directed on page 10. Add to mushroom mixture and cook for 1 more minute; set aside.

In a large bowl, beat together eggs and ricotta cheese. Change to shredding disc and shred jack cheese as directed on page 8. Stir jack cheese, spinach, dill weed, pepper, and mushroom mixture into ricotta mixture. Pour into a greased 10-inch quiche dish or pie pan and bake in a 325° oven until center feels set when lightly touched (35 to 40 minutes). Let cool for 10 minutes, then cut into wedges and serve hot. (Or serve at room temperature.) Makes 6 to 8 servings.

More than Hash

The word "hash" is derived from the French *hache*, meaning ax. We find the food processor to be a far more suitable tool for chopping, though. Here, it prepares ham, potatoes, and cheese for a hearty supper dish.

- 1 **large onion**
- 4 **tablespoons butter or margarine**
- 1 **cup lightly packed parsley sprigs**
- ¾ **pound cooked ham, trimmed of fat and cut into chunks**
- ¾ **pound thin-skinned potatoes, cooked and cooled**
- 8 **ounces Cheddar cheese**
- ¼ **teaspoon liquid hot pepper seasoning**
- 6 **eggs**
- 2 **tablespoons Dijon mustard**
- 2 **cups cubed, toasted bread or plain croutons**

Insert metal blade. Chop onion as directed on page 13. In a wide frying pan with an ovenproof handle, melt 2 tablespoons of the butter over medium heat. Add onion and cook, stirring occasionally, until soft. Meanwhile, chop parsley as directed on page 15. Add to onion and cook for 1 minute. Remove pan from heat.

Chop ham as directed on page 10; add to onion mixture. Cut potatoes into quarters (or eighths if large) and place in work bowl. Process, using on-off pulses, until coarsely chopped. Add to onion mixture. Change to shredding disc and shred cheese as directed on page 8; add cheese and hot pepper seasoning to onion mixture. Mix well, then spread evenly in pan. Make 6 evenly spaced depressions in hash mixture; carefully break an egg into each.

Melt remaining 2 tablespoons butter in a small pan over medium-low heat; stir in mustard, then mix with bread cubes. Sprinkle in a circle around eggs. Bake, uncovered, in a 325° oven until eggs are set to your liking (20 to 30 minutes). Serve immediately. Makes 6 servings.

RECIPE CONVERSION

One benefit of owning a food processor is learning to use it for your favorite nonprocessor recipes. The processor can streamline the preparation of any recipe involving a fair amount of slicing, chopping, or shredding.

Conversion of recipes from conventional to processor style is quite easy. The object is to change blades as little as possible without washing the work bowl between steps.

As you read a conventional recipe, regroup preparation steps so foods needing the same blade are processed sequentially, with dry ingredients processed before wet. In Mushroom-Pepperoni Pizza (page 82), you make the dough first, leaving the work bowl clean and dry for chopping garlic and onions (still using the metal blade). You change to the slicing disc and process bell pepper and mushrooms, then change discs a final time to shred cheese.

Ingredients with similar textures can be chopped at the same time if they'll be used simultaneously in a recipe. For example, in Pork Sui Mai (page 23), you chop tender, crunchy vegetables together, then add them all at once to pork. But carrots and parsley (one hard, one soft) can't be chopped together.

Many conventional recipes call for ingredients in cups (1 cup shredded cheese, 3 cups sliced apples). If you're using the processor, though, it's more helpful to know the amount of food you need *before* processing—4 ounces cheese, 3 small apples. To help you in recipe conversion, the charts on pages 8 to 15 state processing yields in cup amounts.

Party-size Green Onion Quiche

Baked in a large rectangular pan, this thin, oniony quiche easily serves a crowd; you can cut it into big triangles for a main course, or dozens of bite-size squares for appetizers.

- 5 ounces Parmesan cheese
- 2 cloves garlic
- 32 medium-size green onions (4 or 5 bunches)
- ¼ cup butter or margarine
- 8 ounces Swiss cheese
- 12 eggs
- ½ cup whipping cream or sour cream
- ½ teaspoon salt
- ¼ teaspoon each pepper and ground nutmeg

Insert metal blade. Grate Parmesan cheese as directed on page 8; set aside.

Mince garlic as directed on page 13; leave in work bowl. Change to slicing disc and slice onions as directed on page 13. Melt butter in a wide frying pan over medium heat. Add onions and garlic and cook, stirring, just until onions are soft (about 5 minutes). Remove from heat and set aside.

Change to shredding disc and shred Swiss cheese as directed on page 8.

In a large bowl, lightly beat eggs with cream, salt, pepper, and nutmeg. Stir in 1½ cups of the Swiss cheese, half the Parmesan, and onion mixture. Pour into a well-buttered 10 by 15-inch rimmed baking pan. Sprinkle with remaining Parmesan.

Bake in a 350° oven until center feels set when lightly touched (18 to 20 minutes). Sprinkle remaining Swiss cheese on top and return to oven until cheese is melted (about 1 more minute). Let cool slightly on a rack, then cut into large triangles or 1¼-inch squares. Makes 8 to 10 main-dish servings or 8 dozen appetizers.

Party-size Broccoli Quiche

Follow directions for **Party-size Green Onion Quiche,** but omit green onions. Instead, chop 1 large **onion** (see page 13); set aside. Peel stems from 2 pounds **broccoli.** Separate stems and flowerets; cut stems into chunks. Place flowerets in work bowl; process, using on-off pulses, until finely chopped. Set aside. Repeat with stems. Cook onion and garlic in butter until onion is soft, then add broccoli. Cover and cook until tender (about 7 minutes). Substitute ½ teaspoon each **dry mustard** and **dry basil** for nutmeg.

Crab Quiche

This delicate quiche combines seasoned crab in a custard enriched with two cheeses.

- Buttery pastry shell (recipe follows)
- 2 tablespoons lightly packed parsley sprigs
- 2 ounces Swiss, Samsoe, or Gruyère cheese
- 1 large green onion
- 3 tablespoons grated Parmesan cheese (see page 8)
- 6 ounces (about 1½ cups) cooked crabmeat (if frozen, thaw and pat dry)
- ⅛ teaspoon ground red pepper (cayenne)
- 2 eggs
- ¾ cup half-and-half (light cream)
- Paprika

Prepare pastry shell; set aside.

Insert metal blade. Chop parsley as directed on page 15 and transfer to a mixing bowl. Change to shredding disc and shred Swiss cheese as directed on page 8; evenly sprinkle over bottom of shell. Change to slicing disc and slice onion as directed on page 13. Add onion, Parmesan cheese, crabmeat, and pepper to parsley; mix gently and spoon over Swiss cheese.

In a bowl, beat eggs with half-and-half and pour over crab mixture. Sprinkle lightly with paprika. Bake on lowest rack in a 350° oven until custard appears set when dish is gently shaken (about 45 minutes). Let stand for 10 minutes, then cut into wedges. Makes 3 or 4 servings.

Buttery pastry shell. Insert metal blade. Place ¾ cup **all-purpose flour** and 5 tablespoons **butter** or margarine (cut into chunks) in work bowl. Process continuously until mixture resembles fine crumbs. Add 1 **egg yolk** to work bowl; process, using on-off pulses, just until mixture begins to hold together (don't let it form a ball). Work dough into a ball with your hands.

Evenly press dough over bottom and up sides of an 8-inch quiche dish or pie pan, making it flush with rim (dough tears easily; pinch any tears together to rejoin).

Mushroom-filled Oven Pancake

⊙ ⊖ ♫ Adding mushrooms, onion, and seasonings to an oven pancake makes it a substantial treat for a family supper. The pancake batter puffs up when it bakes, and stays puffy when you serve it. If you don't have a wide frying pan with an ovenproof handle, you can prepare the filling as directed, then transfer it to a shallow 3-quart baking dish. (Don't use a heatproof glass dish; it may crack when batter is added.)

4 ounces Cheddar cheese
2 green onions
½ pound mushrooms
1 small onion
  About 7 tablespoons butter or margarine
1 teaspoon dry basil
½ teaspoon salt
⅛ teaspoon *each* pepper and ground nutmeg
4 eggs
1 cup all-purpose flour
1 cup milk
  Sour cream

Preheat oven to 425°.

Insert shredding disc. Shred cheese as directed on page 8; set aside.

Change to slicing disc. Slice green onions as directed on page 13; transfer to a small serving bowl and set aside. Slice mushrooms as directed on page 13; set aside. Change to metal blade and chop onion as directed on page 13.

In a 10-inch frying pan with an ovenproof handle, melt 3 tablespoons of the butter over medium heat. Add chopped onion and mushrooms and cook, stirring occasionally, until onion is soft. Stir in basil, salt, pepper, and nutmeg. Tip pan to estimate drippings, then add more butter (about 4 tablespoons) to make about 5 tablespoons total. Place pan in oven until butter is melted and bubbly. (Or scrape mixture into a shallow 3-quart baking dish, then place in oven.)

Meanwhile, place eggs and flour in work bowl. With motor running, gradually pour milk through feed tube; continue processing for 30 seconds after the last addition.

Remove pan from oven and quickly pour in batter. Sprinkle with cheese and return to oven. Bake until puffy and well browned (20 to 25 minutes). Serve immediately; pass sour cream and green onions at the table. Makes 4 servings.

Zucchini Custard Torte

⊙ ♫ ⊖ An unusual savory streusel mixture is both crust and topping for this torte. Serve it warm or cooled as a brunch or supper entrée, with grilled sausages and a crisp green salad.

5 ounces Swiss cheese
4 ounces Parmesan cheese
  Savory streusel (recipe on page 57)
2 cloves garlic
1 medium-size onion
1 small red or green bell pepper, seeded
5 medium-size zucchini (about 2 lbs. *total*)
2 tablespoons butter or margarine
¼ cup lightly packed fresh basil leaves or 1 teaspoon dry basil
4 eggs
1 cup sour cream

Insert shredding disc. Shred Swiss cheese as directed on page 8; set aside. Change to metal blade. Grate Parmesan cheese as directed on page 8; set aside. Prepare savory streusel, using ¾ cup of the shredded Swiss and ¼ cup of the grated Parmesan. Combine remaining cheeses and set aside. Reserve 1 cup of the streusel; press remainder over bottom and 2 inches up sides of a greased 9-inch spring-form pan.

Mince garlic as directed on page 13; leave in work bowl. Chop onion as directed on page 13; set onion and garlic aside. Chop bell pepper as directed on page 15; leave in work bowl. Change to slicing disc and slice zucchini as directed on page 15. Melt butter in a wide frying pan over medium-high heat. Add zucchini, pepper, onion, and garlic. Cook, stirring, until zucchini is very tender to bite (10 to 12 minutes). Remove from heat.

Change to metal blade and chop fresh basil as directed for parsley on page 15. Transfer to a large mixing bowl and add eggs and sour cream; lightly beat together, then add reserved Swiss and Parmesan cheeses. Stir in zucchini mixture. Spoon into prepared pan; sprinkle reserved streusel evenly over top.

Bake, uncovered, in a 375° oven until torte is puffy and center no longer jiggles when pan is gently shaken (about 45 minutes). Let cool on a rack for about 25 minutes. Run a knife blade around edge, then remove pan sides. Serve warm or at room temperature, cut into wedges. Makes 6 to 8 servings.

(Continued on page 57)

Nothing beats the flavor of homemade butter. And in the processor, it takes only minutes to prepare. Flavored butters are quick to make, too; homemade or purchased butter is the starting point. For a simple appetizer, offer one or more savory butters with bread rounds; the sweet butters make breakfast toast or pancakes extra special.

Store butters covered in the refrigerator for up to 1 week. For easiest spreading and best flavor, serve at room temperature.

Fresh Butter

  2 cups whipping cream, at room temperature
1½ cups cold water
     Salt (optional)

Insert metal blade; place cream in work bowl. Process continuously until cream separates into buttermilk and fluffy clumps of butter (1½ to 2 minutes). Pour mixture through a wire strainer into a bowl. Press gently with a rubber scraper to extract liquid.

Return butter to work bowl; add ½ cup of the water. Process continuously until well mixed. Strain, pressing gently with rubber scraper; discard liquid. Repeat washing and straining 2 more times, using ½ cup water each time. For the final straining, gently press out *all* remaining liquid with scraper.

Place butter in a bowl; season to taste with salt, if desired. Makes 1 cup (½ lb.).

Camembert Butter. Insert metal blade. Place 4 ounces **Camembert** (cut into chunks) in work bowl; add a dash of **ground red pepper** (cayenne), ⅛ teaspoon **white pepper,** and ¼ teaspoon **thyme leaves.** Cut 1 cup (½ lb.) **butter** into 16 chunks. With motor running, drop butter through feed tube, one chunk at a time; continue processing (stopping to scrape bowl once or twice) until fluffy. Makes 1½ cups.

Herb Garlic Butter. Insert metal blade. Mince 2 cloves **garlic** as directed on page 13; leave in work bowl. Add 1 teaspoon **lemon juice** and ½ cup lightly packed **fresh basil or watercress leaves, or parsley sprigs.** Cut ½ cup (¼ lb.) **butter** into 8 chunks. With motor running, drop butter through feed tube, one chunk at a time; continue processing (stopping to scrape bowl once or twice) until mixture is smoothly blended. Makes ⅔ cup.

Smoked Salmon Butter. Insert metal blade. Place ½ cup (4 oz.) **smoked salmon** (cut into chunks) in work bowl. Cut ¾ cup (¼ lb. plus ¼ cup) **butter** into 12 chunks. With motor running, drop butter through feed tube, one chunk at a time; continue processing (stopping to scrape bowl once or twice) until salmon is chopped and mixture is blended. Makes 1½ cups.

Date-Nut Butter. Insert metal blade. Place 3 tablespoons *each* **powdered sugar** and **pitted dates** in work bowl; add ¼ cup **walnuts.** Cut ½ cup (¼ lb.) **butter** into 8 chunks. With motor running, drop butter through feed tube, one chunk at a time; continue processing (stopping to scrape bowl once or twice) until nuts are chopped and mixture is blended. Makes 1 cup.

Orange Spice Butter. Insert metal blade. Place ¼ cup **orange marmalade** in work bowl; add ⅛ teaspoon **ground nutmeg** and ¼ teaspoon *each* **ground ginger** and **ground cinnamon.** Cut ½ cup (¼ lb.) **butter** into 8 chunks. With motor running, drop butter through feed tube, one chunk at a time; continue processing (stopping to scrape bowl once) until mixture is smoothly blended. Makes ¾ cup.

Savory streusel. Insert metal blade. Place 1 cup *each* **whole wheat flour** and **quick-cooking rolled oats** in work bowl. Add ¾ cup of the shredded **Swiss cheese** and ¼ cup of the grated **Parmesan cheese;** process just to combine. Add ½ cup (¼ lb.) **butter** or margarine (cut into chunks) and process continuously just until even crumbs form.

Chunky Cheddar Fondue

A change of pace from the classic Swiss fireside treat, our fondue combines south-of-the-border flavors with a selection of fresh and crunchy dippers.

    Assorted raw vegetables (suggestions follow)
 1 pound Cheddar cheese
 1 medium-size onion
 1 can (about 8 oz.) stewed tomatoes
 3 tablespoons butter or margarine
 1 can (4 oz.) diced green chiles, drained well
 ¼ teaspoon oregano leaves
    Tortilla chips, firm French bread cubes, or
    bread sticks

Prepare vegetables; set aside.

Insert shredding disc. Shred cheese as directed on page 8; set aside. Change to metal blade and chop onion as directed on page 13; set aside. Drain tomatoes, reserving liquid. Place tomatoes in work bowl; process, using on-off pulses, until chopped.

Melt butter in a 10-inch frying pan over medium heat. Add onion and cook, stirring occasionally, until lightly browned (about 10 minutes). Add tomatoes and reserved liquid, chiles, and oregano. Reduce heat and simmer, uncovered, for 5 minutes. Add cheese, a handful at a time, stirring until cheese is melted and mixture is well blended.

If desired, transfer to a fondue pot or chafing dish and keep warm over heat source. Use vegetables and chips as dippers. Makes 3 cups (3 or 4 servings).

Assorted raw vegetables. You'll need 6 to 8 cups vegetables. Choose from the following: **green or red bell pepper** strips, **carrot** sticks or whole baby carrots, **zucchini** rounds, **celery** sticks, **mushrooms** (quartered if large), **green onions, cauliflower** flowerets.

Ricotta Gnocchi with Pesto

Gnocchi (literally, "lumps") are a traditional Italian dumpling-like pasta equivalent. Like pasta, gnocchi lend themselves to variations; the dough can be made with potatoes, spinach, polenta—or with ricotta cheese, as in our recipe. Top the little bow-shaped dumplings with butter and Parmesan cheese or basil-scented pesto.

    Pesto (page 106)
 1 clove garlic
 ¼ cup grated Parmesan cheese (see page 8)
 2 cups ricotta cheese
 2 eggs
 1 teaspoon salt
 2 cups all-purpose flour
 5 quarts water
    Butter
    Salt and pepper

Prepare Pesto; set aside.

Insert metal blade. Mince garlic as directed on page 13; leave in work bowl. Add Parmesan cheese, ricotta cheese, eggs, salt, and flour to work bowl; process continuously (stopping to scrape bowl once or twice) until mixture forms a ball. Dust dough lightly with flour, wrap in plastic wrap, and refrigerate until slightly firm (4 to 6 hours).

Place dough on a lightly floured board. With your hands, roll small pieces of dough into ⅜-inch-thick ropes; cut ropes into 1¼-inch lengths. Place your forefinger on the center of each length; roll lightly to form a bow-shaped dumpling. Set gnocchi slightly apart on wax-paper-lined baking sheets. (At this point, you may cover and refrigerate gnocchi until next day. Or freeze on baking sheets until firm, then transfer to plastic bags and store in freezer for up to 1 month. Do not thaw before cooking.)

To cook, bring water to a boil in a 6 to 8-quart kettle over high heat. Drop 30 to 40 gnocchi at a time into kettle. When water returns to a boil, adjust heat so water boils very gently. Cook, uncovered, until gnocchi are cooked throughout (about 10 minutes, about 12 minutes if frozen; sample a dumpling to test).

Drain cooked gnocchi briefly, then keep hot in a covered dish. When all are cooked, season to taste with butter, salt, and pepper. Top each serving with about 2 tablespoons Pesto. Makes 6 to 8 servings.

Meats, Poultry & Seafood

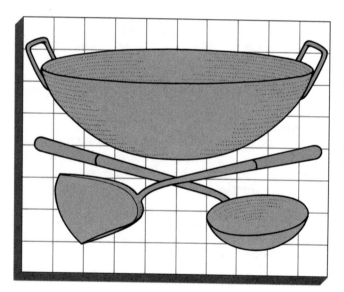

Sausage & Vegetable Patties

These pork sausage patties are all dressed up for supper—they're crunchy with chopped vegetables and spiked with chili sauce. Serve them on rye bread or toasted English muffins.

- 1 *each* small onion and green bell pepper (seeded)
- 1 small carrot, cut into 1-inch chunks
- ¼ cup lightly packed parsley sprigs
- 1 pound bulk pork sausage
- ⅓ cup fine dry bread crumbs (see page 10)
  Tomato-based chili sauce
- 1 egg
- ¼ teaspoon *each* pepper, garlic salt, and rubbed sage

Insert metal blade. Following directions on pages 13 and 15, chop onion and transfer to a large mixing bowl; then chop bell pepper and add to bowl. Place carrot in work bowl; process, using on-off pulses, until chopped. Add to mixing bowl. Finely chop parsley as directed on page 15; add to mixing bowl with sausage, bread crumbs, 2 tablespoons chili sauce, egg, pepper, garlic salt, and sage. Mix until blended. Shape mixture into 6 round patties, each ¾ to 1 inch thick.

Heat a 12 to 14-inch frying pan with a nonstick finish over medium heat. Add patties and cook, turning as needed, until browned on outside and no longer pink when slashed (6 to 7 minutes per side). Serve with additional chili sauce, if desired. Makes 6 servings.

Lamb Pocket Burgers

These burgers have a definite Middle Eastern accent. You cook the curry-seasoned lamb patties on the grill, then slip them into warmed pocket bread halves and top with cucumber, chutney, and yogurt.

Condiments (directions follow)
1 small onion
⅓ cup dried apricots
¼ cup fine dry bread crumbs (see page 10)
1 pound lean ground lamb, purchased or ground in the processor (see page 10)
1 egg
2 teaspoons curry powder
3 pocket breads, cut in half

Prepare condiments and set aside.

Insert metal blade. Chop onion as directed on page 13; set aside. Place apricots in work bowl and process, using on-off pulses, until chopped. Leave in work bowl. Add onion, bread crumbs, lamb, egg, and curry powder; process, using on-off pulses, until ingredients are well combined.

Shape mixture into 6 oblong patties, each 3 to 4 inches long and about ½ inch thick. Place patties on a lightly greased grill, 4 to 6 inches above a solid bed of glowing coals. Cook, turning as needed, until done to your liking when slashed— about 10 minutes total for medium-rare. (Or broil 3 inches below heat for 4 to 5 minutes per side.)

While patties cook, wrap pocket breads in heavy-duty foil and heat at side of grill, if desired. (If broiling patties, place breads in oven during last few minutes of cooking.)

To serve, place each patty in a pocket bread half and top with condiments. Makes 6 servings.

Condiments. Insert slicing disc. Slice 1 medium-size **cucumber** as directed on page 13; place in a small bowl. Change to metal blade; place ¼ to ½ cup **Major Grey's chutney** in work bowl and process, using on-off pulses, until chopped. Place in a small bowl. Pass **plain yogurt** in a third bowl.

Individual Meat Loaves

Single-serving-size meat loaves tuck neatly inside sandwich rolls for a picnic or light supper entrée. A spiced catsup mixture tops each loaf, cooking into the meat during baking. Serve raw vegetables and dip alongside, then finish with fresh fruit and cookies.

1 clove garlic
½ cup lightly packed parsley sprigs
½ cup green onion pieces (white part only, cut into 1-inch lengths)
1 pound cooked ham, trimmed of fat and cut into chunks
½ pound lean, boneless pork, trimmed of fat and cut into chunks
2 eggs
3 tablespoons lemon juice
¼ cup milk
3 sandwich-size slices bread, cut into ½-inch squares
½ cup catsup
⅓ cup firmly packed brown sugar
1 teaspoon dry mustard
¼ teaspoon each ground allspice and cloves
6 thin lemon slices (see page 9)

Insert metal blade. Mince garlic as directed on page 13; leave in work bowl. Add parsley and onion pieces; process, using on-off pulses, until chopped. Leave in work bowl. Add half each of ham and pork to work bowl; grind as directed on page 10, stopping to scrape bowl once. Set aside. Repeat with remaining ham and pork. (Or grind meat all at once in a large-capacity processor.) Set meat mixture aside.

Break eggs into work bowl. Process continuously until well combined. Add lemon juice, milk, and bread; process just to moisten bread, using on-off pulses. Return all meat mixture to work bowl. Process, using on-off pulses, until ingredients are well combined. Cover and refrigerate until firm enough to shape (about 15 minutes).

Divide meat mixture into 6 equal portions; shape each into a 5-inch-long log. Place logs 2 inches apart on a rimmed baking sheet. Bake in a 350° oven for 15 minutes.

Stir together catsup, sugar, mustard, allspice, and cloves. Drizzle catsup mixture evenly over loaves, then top each with a lemon slice. Bake, uncovered, until centers feel firm when pressed (about 30 more minutes). Let cool for at least 10 minutes before serving. Makes 6 servings.

Sweet & Sour Meatballs

This recipe calls for lots of slicing and chopping—but if you use your food processor, preparation is a snap.

1 small green bell pepper, seeded
2 medium-size carrots
2 medium-size stalks celery
1 can (8 oz.) water chestnuts, drained well
Sesame oven meatballs (recipe follows)
2 tablespoons cornstarch
½ cup firmly packed brown sugar
¼ teaspoon ground ginger
¼ teaspoon crushed red pepper (optional)
2 tablespoons *each* soy sauce and dry sherry
½ cup *each* wine vinegar and regular-strength beef broth
2 tablespoons salad oil
1 can (8 oz.) pineapple chunks in their own juice, drained well
Hot cooked rice or noodles

Insert slicing disc. Slice bell pepper, then carrots, then celery as directed on pages 15 and 12; set vegetables aside. Stack water chestnuts, flat sides down, in feed tube; slice. Set aside.

Prepare meatballs. While meatballs bake, combine cornstarch, sugar, ginger, red pepper (if used), soy, sherry, vinegar, and broth; set aside.

Heat oil in a wok or wide frying pan over high heat. Add bell pepper, carrots, and celery; stir-fry for 2 minutes. Add water chestnuts and pineapple and stir-fry until carrots are tender to bite (about 2 more minutes). Pour cornstarch mixture into pan and cook, stirring, until sauce boils and thickens. Add meatballs; stir to coat with sauce. Serve immediately, with rice. Makes 4 servings.

Sesame oven meatballs. Insert metal blade. Mince 1 large clove **garlic** as directed on page 13; leave in work bowl. Add 4 **green onions** (white part only, cut into 1-inch lengths) and chop as directed on page 15. Add ¼ cup **fine dry bread crumbs** (see page 10), ½ cup **milk,** 1 **egg,** ½ teaspoon **salt,** ¼ teaspoon *each* **ground ginger** and **pepper,** 2 tablespoons **sesame seeds,** and ½ pound *each* **lean ground beef** and **lean ground pork.** Process, using on-off pulses, just until evenly combined. Shape mixture into 1-inch balls and place on a rimmed baking sheet. Bake, uncovered, in a 500° oven until no longer pink when slashed (10 to 12 minutes). Remove with a slotted spoon and let drain on paper towels.

Piroshkis

Typically offered with tea or cocktails, traditional Russian piroshkis are small enough to eat in one or two bites. We've devised a larger version, big enough for a lunch or supper entrée. Try serving the plump sandwiches with Sweet & Sour Borscht (page 47).

Egg pastry (page 64)
½ cup lightly packed parsley sprigs
½ pound mushrooms
2 cloves garlic
1 medium-size onion
1 teaspoon salt
1 pound lean ground beef, purchased or ground in the processor (see page 10)
1 teaspoon dill weed
½ cup half-and-half (light cream)
2 hard-cooked eggs
Pepper

Prepare egg pastry; set aside.

Insert metal blade. Following directions on pages 15 and 13, finely chop parsley and set aside; then chop mushrooms and set aside. Mince garlic as directed on page 13 and leave in work bowl, then chop onion.

Sprinkle salt into a wide frying pan over medium-high heat. Crumble beef into pan; cook, stirring, for 2 minutes. Add onion and garlic and cook, stirring, for 5 more minutes. Stir in mushrooms and cook until meat is no longer pink and vegetables are soft (about 5 more minutes). Add dill weed and half-and-half; cook, stirring, until all liquid has evaporated. Remove from heat.

Chop eggs as directed on page 8. Stir eggs and parsley into meat mixture; season to taste with pepper.

Divide pastry in half. Cut each half into 4 equal pieces; then shape each piece into a ball. On a floured board, roll out each ball to a 7-inch round. Place about ½ cup of the filling on half of each round, spreading it to within ½ inch of edges; then lightly moisten edges of dough with water. Fold other half over to enclose filling. Press edges together with a fork to seal; prick top in several places. With a knife, trim excess dough from edge of turnover to form an even half moon.

Using a wide spatula, transfer piroshkis to an ungreased baking sheet, placing them 1 inch apart. Bake in a 425° oven until lightly browned (20 to 25 minutes). Serve warm. Makes 8.

Vegetable & Cheese-stuffed Pork Chops

🌙 ⚙ You make these plump stuffed pork chops in four steps. Cut a pocket in each thick chop and fill it with a savory vegetable mixture; brown the chops briefly in butter, then bake them to juicy perfection. Offer white or wild rice pilaf to complete a company menu.

½ cup lightly packed parsley sprigs
1 clove garlic
1 small onion
1 small inner stalk celery
1 small carrot
4 tablespoons butter or margarine
½ teaspoon marjoram leaves
Dash of pepper
Salt
¾ cup unseasoned croutons
3 tablespoons grated Parmesan cheese (see page 8)
6 large rib or loin pork chops (each about 1 inch thick), trimmed of fat

Insert metal blade. Finely chop parsley as directed on page 15 and set aside. Mince garlic as directed on page 13; leave in work bowl. Chop onion as directed on page 13; add onion and garlic to parsley. Chop celery as directed on page 12; leave in work bowl. Change to shredding disc and shred carrot as directed on page 12.

Melt 2 tablespoons of the butter in a wide frying pan over medium heat. Add carrot, celery, onion, garlic, parsley, marjoram, and pepper. Season to taste with salt. Cook, stirring, until onion is soft. Stir in croutons and cheese. Remove from heat.

With a sharp knife, slash through meat of each chop, almost to bone, to form a pocket. Fill each pocket with about 3 tablespoons of the vegetable-cheese stuffing; fasten pockets closed with metal skewers or wooden picks. (Reserve any remaining stuffing to heat and serve alongside chops.)

Melt remaining 2 tablespoons butter in a wide frying pan over medium heat. Add chops and cook, turning as needed, until well browned on both sides; then place in a single layer in a 9 by 13-inch baking pan. Cover with foil and bake in a 350° oven until meat near bone is no longer pink when slashed (35 to 40 minutes). Makes 6 servings.

Veal with Tuna Sauce

🌙 ⚙ A classic offering for a cold buffet, *vitello tonnato* combines sliced simmered veal with a creamy tuna sauce. If you wish, substitute turkey breast for veal—it's much less costly, and equally tasty.

1 each large carrot and onion
1 large stalk celery
1 clove garlic
1 veal leg or shoulder or 1 turkey breast (4 to 5 lbs.), boned, rolled, and tied
1½ cups dry white wine
1 bay leaf
6 parsley sprigs
Tuna sauce (recipe follows)
Lemon slices (see page 9), capers, and parsley sprigs

Insert slicing disc. Following directions on pages 12 and 13, slice carrot, then onion, then celery; place vegetables in a 5 to 6-quart kettle.

Change to metal blade. Mince garlic as directed on page 13; add to kettle with veal, wine, bay leaf, the 6 parsley sprigs, and just enough water to barely cover meat. Bring to a boil over high heat; then cover, reduce heat, and simmer until meat is tender when pierced or until a meat thermometer registers 170° when inserted in thickest part (1½ to 2 hours). Let meat cool in cooking liquid, then cover and refrigerate until cold. Meanwhile, prepare tuna sauce.

Remove meat from liquid and slice thinly. (Strain liquid for use in soup, if desired; store in refrigerator or freezer.) Pour a third of the tuna sauce into a large, shallow serving dish. Arrange sliced meat in dish and cover with remaining sauce. Cover and refrigerate for at least 2 hours or until next day. Just before serving, garnish with lemon slices, capers, and parsley. Makes about 10 servings.

Tuna sauce. Insert metal blade. Drain oil from 1 small can (about 3 oz.) **tuna packed in oil** into a measuring cup; add enough **olive oil** or salad oil to make 1 cup. Place tuna in work bowl with 5 **anchovy fillets**, 3 tablespoons **lemon juice**, 2 **eggs**, and 1½ tablespoons **capers** (drained well). With motor running, slowly pour oil through feed tube and continue processing until sauce is thick and well blended. If made ahead, cover and refrigerate for up to 1 week.

If you want sausage that tastes just right every time, consider making your own. You can adjust the seasonings to your liking, and you're guaranteed a preservative-free product. To make sausage, you'll need only your processor and some basic utensils (and another person's help to shape links).

Meat & fat. For the juiciest, most flavorful sausage, use equal parts of meat and fat. If you're making pork sausage, there may be enough fat on the meat, but ask for extra pork fat just to be sure.

Separate lean meat from fat, then cut both into 1-inch chunks. (Or just cut pork fat and chicken or veal into 1-inch chunks.) To make grinding easier, refrigerate fat and meat until cold; refrigerate the two separately if recipe directs you to grind them separately.

Casings. To make sausage links, you'll need natural sausage casings (about 1¼ inches in diameter). Order them ahead from a meat market; they come refrigerated, packed in salt. To prepare casings, cut them into 2 to 3-yard sections and soak in tepid water for about 10 minutes. Then slip one end of each section over a smooth-tipped faucet; run cool water through casing to rinse off salt. Return to tepid water and let stand until ready to use. Just before using, drain casings and strip off excess water with your fingers.

Shaping links. Fit a plastic-lined pastry bag with a plain metal tip having an opening at least ½ inch wide. Or fit bag with the plastic part of a gravy baster, tip cut off.

Fill bag two-thirds full with sausage. To fill each section of casing, thread it onto the handle of a rubber scraper. Insert handle into pastry tip, then push casing onto tip so 3 to 4 inches of casing extend over tip onto pastry bag. Remove handle.

Twist pastry bag with even pressure to force sausage through tip into casing. You'll need 2 pairs of hands—one to squeeze out sausage, the other to form links. To form links, twist casing at 6-inch intervals as sausage flows into it. If air bubbles form, prick with a pin to deflate. If casing tears, force meat out through tear with your fingers and tie off casing at that point. Once casing is filled, tie ends; then retwist at links to secure. To cook links, see facing page.

Shaping patties. Pork sausages can be shaped into patties as well as links. Form sausage into ½-inch-thick patties; then stack, placing wax paper between patties for easy separation. (If you plan to use sausage as bulk sausage, shape it into loaves.)

To cook patties, coat a frying pan with melted butter or margarine and set over medium heat. Add patties; cook, turning once or twice, until well browned on both sides.

Boudin Blanc

½ cup lightly packed parsley sprigs

3 large onions

½ pound pork fat, cut into 1-inch chunks

1 cup milk

¾ cup fine dry bread crumbs (see page 10)

1 pound *each* boneless veal and boned, skinned chicken breast, cut into 1-inch chunks

1 teaspoon salt

¼ teaspoon *each* ground nutmeg, ground allspice, and white pepper

2 tablespoons coarsely chopped chives

2 eggs

2 egg whites

½ cup whipping cream

About 4 yards natural sausage casings

Butter or margarine (optional)

Insert metal blade. Finely chop parsley as directed on page 15; set aside. Chop onions as directed on page 13; set aside.

Place fat in work bowl and process continuously until it forms a fine paste. Transfer half the fat to a large bowl; add milk and bread crumbs, stir to blend, and set aside.

Melt remaining fat in a 10 to 12-inch frying pan over medium-low heat (do not let fat brown). Add onions; cook, stirring occasionally, until pale gold (15 to 20 minutes).

Meanwhile, in a large bowl, mix veal and chicken with parsley, salt, nutmeg, allspice, pepper, and chives. Stir in onions. Place half the mixture in work bowl. Process continuously until finely ground, then add 1 of the eggs, 1 of the egg whites, and ¼ cup of the cream; continue processing until well blended. Add to crumb mixture. Repeat with remaining meat mixture, egg, egg white, and cream; add to crumb mixture and beat to blend well.

Shape sausage into links as directed on facing page. To cook, bring 5 quarts water to a boil in an 8-quart kettle over high heat. Turn off heat; at once add sausages. Cover and let stand until sausages feel firm when pressed (25 to 30 minutes). Drain, then cut links apart. Serve sausages as is, or brown them.

To brown links, melt enough butter to coat bottom of a frying pan. Add as many links as desired (without crowding) and cook over medium-low heat, turning, until browned on all sides.

To store sausages, cover and refrigerate for up to 3 days; freeze for longer storage (thaw in refrigerator). Makes about 4½ pounds.

Mild Italian Sausage

4½ pounds boneless pork butt

3 to 5 cloves garlic

2¼ teaspoons *each* fennel seeds and white pepper

1½ teaspoons sage leaves

2½ to 3½ teaspoons salt

¾ cup dry white wine

5 to 6 yards natural sausage casings (optional)

1 tablespoon butter or margarine

Separate lean meat from fat, then cut both into cubes. Measure or weigh; you should have equal parts (2¼ lbs. *each*) fat and meat.

Insert metal blade. Mince garlic as directed on page 13; transfer to a large mixing bowl. Place fat and meat in work bowl, a fourth at a time (or half at a time in a large-capacity processor); process, using on-off pulses, until coarsely ground. Transfer to mixing bowl with fennel seeds, pepper, sage, salt, and wine. Mix well with your hands. Cover and refrigerate for at least 2 hours or until next day. Shape into patties or links.

Sausages have best flavor if allowed to mellow at least overnight before cooking. Wrap airtight and refrigerate for up to 3 days; freeze for longer storage.

To cook patties, follow directions on facing page. To cook links, pour ⅛ inch water into a frying pan; add as many links as desired (don't crowd in pan). Bring to a boil; then cover, reduce heat to low, and simmer for 8 minutes. Drain. Add butter to pan; cook sausages, turning, until well browned. Makes 4½ pounds.

French-style Picnic Pie

𝄞 A variation on the elegant French *pâté en croûte*, this sturdy picnic pie contains deftly seasoned ground meats in a crisp, golden crust. It's a tasty lunch or supper entrée, equally good warm or at room temperature. Complete the meal with a dip and a platter of crudités.

> 2 **cloves garlic**
> ½ **cup lightly packed parsley sprigs**
> 1 **medium-size onion**
> 2 **tablespoons butter or margarine**
> ½ **cup dry white wine**
> ½ **pound cooked ham, trimmed of fat and cut into chunks**
> 1 **sandwich-size slice bread**
> 1 **pound ground veal, ground turkey, or very lean ground beef, purchased or ground in the processor (see page 10)**
> 1 **egg**
> ½ **teaspoon *each* salt, thyme leaves, and dry mustard**
> ¼ **teaspoon ground allspice**
> ⅛ **teaspoon white pepper**
> **Egg pastry (recipe follows)**
> 1 **egg white beaten with 1 teaspoon water**

Insert metal blade. Mince garlic as directed on page 13; set aside. Following directions on pages 15 and 13, finely chop parsley and transfer to a large mixing bowl; then chop onion.

Melt butter in a wide frying pan over medium heat. Add onion and cook, stirring, until soft. Add garlic and wine, bring to a boil, and cook, stirring often, until almost all liquid has evaporated.

Meanwhile, grind ham as directed on page 10; add to parsley. Process bread into crumbs as directed on page 10. Stir crumbs, onion-wine mixture, veal, egg, salt, thyme, mustard, allspice, and pepper into ham-parsley mixture.

Prepare egg pastry. With your hands, shape pastry into 2 balls, one a little larger than the other. On a lightly floured board, roll out larger portion to about a 12-inch circle. Fit into an 8-inch round cake pan (at least 1½ inches deep) with a removable bottom. Trim edge so pastry overhangs pan rim about ½ inch.

Pat meat mixture evenly into crust. Roll out remaining pastry to a 9 to 10-inch circle and place over filling. Moisten edges of pastry, fold overhanging top pastry over bottom edge, and flute to seal. Cut a small air vent in center of top. If desired, roll out pastry trimmings and cut into decorative shapes; arrange on top crust. Brush top crust evenly with egg white mixture.

Place pie on a rimmed baking sheet. Bake on lowest rack in a 375° oven until well browned (about 1 hour).

To serve hot, let cool for at least 15 minutes; then remove pan sides and cut pie into wedges. Or let cool completely, remove pan sides, and serve at room temperature. Makes 6 to 8 servings.

Egg pastry. Insert metal blade. Place 2½ cups **all-purpose flour,** 1½ teaspoons **salt,** ¼ cup **solid vegetable shortening,** and ¼ cup **butter** or margarine (cut into chunks) in work bowl. Process continuously until mixture resembles coarse crumbs. In a measuring cup, beat 1 **egg yolk,** then add enough **cold water** to make ½ cup; beat well. With motor running, pour yolk mixture through feed tube and continue processing just until dough begins to hold together (don't let it form a ball). Gather dough together with your hands.

Molded Moussaka

𝄞 Moussaka is usually presented as a layered casserole of cooked meat and eggplant, but this molded version is a little different. Eggplant skins are roasted, then used to make a shiny purple cloak for a savory filling of lamb and chopped eggplant pulp.

> 2 **medium-size eggplants (about 1 lb. *each*)**
> **Olive oil or salad oil**
> **Lamb & mint filling (recipe follows)**
> **Fresh mint sprigs**
> **Lemon slices (see page 9)**
> 2 **cups plain yogurt**

Quarter eggplants lengthwise to make a total of 8 wedges. Cut pulp out of wedges, leaving shells ¼ to ⅓ inch thick. Reserve pulp for filling.

Lightly rub skin sides of shells with oil; then arrange shells, cut side down, on a lightly oiled baking sheet. Bake, uncovered, in a 450° oven until skins feel very soft when pressed (35 to 40 minutes). Loosen from baking sheet and let cool slightly. While shells bake, prepare filling.

To assemble, arrange baked shells in an oiled 9-inch round cake pan, skin side down and radiating out from center of pan. Spoon filling evenly into pan and fold any overhanging shell ends over filling. (At this point, you may cover and refrigerate until next day.)

Set pan on a rimmed baking sheet to catch drips. Bake, uncovered, in a 400° oven until hot throughout (about 45 minutes; 55 minutes if refrigerated). Let stand for 10 minutes. To unmold, invert a serving dish over cake pan; holding dish in place, carefully invert both. Shake firmly to loosen moussaka from pan; lift off pan. Let cool for at least 10 minutes. Serve warm or at room temperature, cut into wedges and garnished with mint and lemon slices. Pass yogurt at the table. Makes 8 servings.

Lamb & mint filling. Insert metal blade. Chop 1 cup lightly packed **fresh mint leaves** as directed for parsley on page 15; set aside. Mince 3 cloves **garlic** as directed on page 13 and leave in work bowl. Chop 2 large **onions** as directed on page 13; set onions and garlic aside. Chop 1 large **green bell pepper** (seeded) as directed on page 15. Set aside.

Cut reserved **eggplant pulp** into 1½-inch chunks. Place in work bowl, a quarter at a time (or half at a time in a large-capacity processor); process, using on-off pulses, until chopped.

Heat ¼ cup **olive oil** or salad oil in a 12-inch frying pan over medium heat. Add eggplant, onions, and garlic. Cover and cook, stirring often, until eggplant mashes easily (about 20 minutes).

Meanwhile, coarsely grind 1½ pounds **lean, boneless lamb** as directed on page 10. Add lamb and ¼ teaspoon **pepper** to eggplant mixture. Increase heat to medium-high; cook, breaking up meat with a spoon, until juices have evaporated (10 to 15 minutes). Blend in 3 tablespoons **all-purpose flour;** then add bell pepper, mint, and ¼ cup **plain yogurt.** Cook, stirring, until bubbly. Remove from heat and stir in 2 tablespoons **lemon juice.** Season to taste with **salt.**

Liver on Crisp Potato Pancake

⊗ ⊖ ⊗ Liver and onions take on a new dimension when tossed with a creamy mustard sauce and served over a giant potato pancake. The secret to success with this dish is to cook the liver briefly—just enough to brown the outside but keep the inside moist and pink.

½ **cup lightly packed parsley sprigs**
1 **small onion**
4 **strips bacon**
1 **pound russet potatoes**
1 **tablespoon all-purpose flour**
4 **tablespoons butter or margarine**
½ **pound calf's liver (membrane removed), cut into ¼-inch strips; or ½ pound chicken livers, cut in half**
2 **teaspoons Dijon mustard**
¼ **cup whipping cream**
  Lemon wedges

Insert metal blade. Finely chop parsley as directed on page 15; set aside. Change to slicing disc. Slice onion as directed on page 13 and set aside.

In a 10-inch frying pan with a nonstick finish, cook bacon over medium heat until crisp; lift out, drain, crumble, and set aside. Pour off and reserve drippings, but don't wash pan.

Change to shredding disc. Peel potatoes, then shred as directed on page 15. Immediately drop shredded potatoes into a large bowl of cold water; stir gently, then drain well. Wipe bowl dry; return potatoes to bowl; add flour, and mix well.

Melt 1 tablespoon of the butter in pan used for bacon over medium heat. Add potato mixture and pat into an even layer. Cover and cook for 5 minutes. Uncover and continue to cook until bottom is browned; press firmly with a wide spatula to compact.

Slide pancake onto a flat plate or pan lid. Melt 1 more tablespoon butter in pan; invert pancake into pan so browned side is up. Cook until browned on bottom, then slide onto a warm serving plate. Keep hot.

Pour 1 tablespoon of the reserved drippings into pan. Add onion and cook, stirring, until soft (5 to 7 minutes); set aside on a rimmed plate.

Pour 1 more teaspoon drippings into pan. Add liver and cook, turning as needed, until browned on outside but still pink in center (1 to 2 minutes). Set aside with onions.

Add 2 more tablespoons drippings to pan along with remaining 2 tablespoons butter, mustard, and cream. Increase heat to high; cook, stirring, until sauce forms large, shiny bubbles. Add any liver juices that have collected on plate; boil until thickened again. Add liver, onions, and parsley to sauce and stir just until heated through.

Spoon liver mixture onto potato pancake; top with bacon. Garnish with lemon wedges. Makes 3 or 4 servings.

Simmered Brisket with Vegetables

⊖ ♫ ☺ Gentle simmering cooks thrifty brisket to tenderness in this one-dish meal—perfect for supper on a chilly winter's eve.

3 medium-size carrots
2 medium-size turnips, peeled and quartered
1⅓ cups lightly packed parsley sprigs
1 large onion
1 lean fresh beef brisket (5 to 6 lbs.)
3 to 4 pounds beef soup bones, sawed into 3 to 4-inch pieces
10 cups water
3 beef bouillon cubes
2 bay leaves
1½ teaspoons *each* dry rosemary and thyme leaves
½ teaspoon whole black peppercorns
10 to 12 small thin-skinned potatoes, *each* 2 to 3 inches in diameter
1½ pounds green beans (ends removed), cut in half if large
2 small Golden Delicious apples
2 tablespoons white wine vinegar
½ cup prepared horseradish

Insert slicing disc. Slice carrots as directed on page 12; leave in work bowl. Place turnips vertically in feed tube; slice. Set turnips and carrots aside. Change to metal blade. Finely chop parsley as directed on page 15; set aside. Chop onion as directed on page 13.

Trim and discard excess fat from brisket, then place in an 8 to 10-quart kettle. Cook over medium heat, turning as needed, until well browned on all sides. Lift out and set aside. Add onion, turnips, and carrots to drippings. Cook, stirring, until onion is soft and lightly browned. Return brisket to kettle with beef bones, parsley, water, bouillon cubes, bay leaves, rosemary, thyme, and peppercorns. Bring to a boil; then cover, reduce heat, and simmer until meat is very tender when pierced—2½ to 3 hours. (At this point, you may let cool, then cover and refrigerate until next day.)

Skim and discard fat from broth. (Or lift off and discard solidified fat from refrigerated broth, then place over medium heat until hot—about 25 minutes.) Add potatoes and cook, covered, for 15 minutes. Add beans; continue to cook, covered, until potatoes are tender throughout when pierced (about 10 more minutes). Lift meat to a platter and surround with vegetables; keep hot. Discard bones (reserve broth for another meal).

Insert shredding disc. Core apples and cut in half; stack halves in feed tube and shred. Mix apples with vinegar and transfer to a small serving bowl.

To serve, slice meat; offer apples and horseradish at the table to accompany meat and vegetables. Makes 8 to 10 servings.

Stir-fried Beef with Vegetables

⊖ ♫ A gingery wine-soy marinade both tenderizes sliced lean beef and imparts a wonderful flavor to the finished dish.

1 pound lean, boneless beef (such as top round or sirloin), frozen until firm
1 clove garlic
1 quarter-size slice fresh ginger
¼ cup dry red wine
2 tablespoons soy sauce
½ pound mushrooms
5 green onions
1 large stalk celery
1 can (8 oz.) water chestnuts, drained well
2 tablespoons salad oil
2 tablespoons hoisin sauce
Fresh cilantro (coriander) sprigs

Insert slicing disc. Partially thaw beef until it passes the knife test (see page 9); then slice as directed on same page. Transfer to a bowl.

Change to metal blade. Mince garlic, then ginger as directed on page 13; add to meat with wine and soy. Stir to mix well. Cover and refrigerate for 2 to 4 hours.

Change to slicing disc. Following directions on pages 13 and 12, slice mushrooms, then onions, then celery; set all aside. Stack water chestnuts, flat sides down, in feed tube; slice.

Heat a wok or 12-inch frying pan over high heat. When pan is hot, add oil; then add meat and marinade and stir-fry until meat is no longer red (about 2 minutes). Lift out meat and set aside on a plate. At once add water chestnuts, mushrooms, onions, celery, and hoisin to pan; stir-fry until celery is tender-crisp to bite (2 to 3 minutes). Return meat and juices to pan; stir until heated through. Spoon onto a platter and garnish with cilantro. Serve at once. Makes 4 servings.

Good cooks everywhere know that sauces add flair and flavor to a meal. And with a processor, they're quick and practically foolproof to prepare.

Try classic hollandaise over tender-crisp steamed vegetables (such as asparagus), or as a golden crown for poached fish or eggs Benedict. Our pimento version of *beurre blanc* (a butter-finished reduction sauce) has a smooth, rich flavor and color; it's a perfect accompaniment to seafood or poultry. Pucia-Pucia, a savory herb sauce, adds fragrance and flavor to grilled meats.

Hollandaise Sauce

- 1 egg, at room temperature
- 1 teaspoon Dijon mustard
- 1 tablespoon lemon juice
- 1 cup (½ lb.) butter or margarine, melted and hot (about 160°)

Insert metal blade. Place egg, mustard, and lemon juice in work bowl. With motor running, pour hot melted butter through feed tube in a slow, steady stream. Continue processing until sauce is foamy and slightly thickened (about 2 minutes). Serve immediately. Or, if made ahead, pour into a jar, cover, and let stand for up to 1 hour at room temperature. To reheat, place jar in water that's hot to the touch; stir sauce until it's warm (not hot). Makes about 1 cup.

Pimento Beurre Blanc

- 1 can (7 oz.) whole pimentos, drained well
- ¼ cup dry white wine
- ½ cup regular-strength chicken broth
- ¼ teaspoon dry basil
- ½ cup (¼ lb.) butter or margarine, melted and hot (about 160°)

Insert metal blade. Place pimentos and wine in work bowl; process continuously until smooth. Scrape mixture into a wide frying pan. Add broth and basil. Bring to a boil over high heat; then boil, stirring, until reduced to about ¾ cup. Place mixture in work bowl. With motor running, pour hot melted butter through feed tube in a slow, steady stream; continue processing until combined. Serve immediately, or reheat as directed for Hollandaise Sauce. Makes 1¼ cups.

Pucia-Pucia

- 1 clove garlic
- ¼ cup lightly packed parsley sprigs
- 2 tablespoons fresh sage leaves
- 4 teaspoons fresh rosemary
- 1 tablespoon fresh oregano leaves
- 2 teaspoons fresh thyme leaves
- 2 tablespoons olive oil or salad oil
- 2 tablespoons *each* soy sauce and Worcestershire
- ¼ teaspoon pepper

Insert metal blade. Mince garlic as directed on page 13; leave in work bowl. Add parsley, sage, rosemary, oregano, and thyme; chop as directed for parsley on page 15. Add oil, soy, Worcestershire, and pepper. Process, using on-off pulses (stopping to scrape bowl once), until combined.

Use pucia-pucia as a baste and sauce for grilled chicken, ribs, or steaks. Five minutes before removing meat from grill, brush liberally on all sides with sauce. Pour any remaining sauce over meat when served. Makes about ½ cup, enough for 3 to 4 pounds of meat.

Chicken with a Pocketful of Mushrooms

∮ A pocket cut in a boneless chicken breast makes a handy container for sautéed shiitake mushrooms. Fresh shiitake mushrooms are sometimes available in Asian and specialty produce markets; if you can't find them, use regular mushrooms.

  3 whole chicken breasts, skinned, boned, and split
  1 quarter-size slice fresh ginger
     Sautéed mushrooms (recipe follows)
  3 tablespoons butter or margarine
  6 large fresh shiitake mushrooms or regular mushrooms
  ⅓ cup dry sherry
  1 cup regular-strength chicken broth
  1½ tablespoons soy sauce
  ½ teaspoon *each* sugar and vinegar
  1 tablespoon cornstarch mixed with 2 tablespoons water

Gently pull off slim fillet on inside of each breast half; set fillets aside. In thickest part of each half, cut a 3½-inch-long pocket, about 2 inches deep.

Insert metal blade. Mince ginger as directed on page 13; set aside.

Prepare sautéed mushrooms; tuck 2 to 3 tablespoons into pocket in each breast half. (At this point, you may cover and refrigerate fillets and filled breasts until next day.)

Melt butter in a 12 to 14-inch frying pan over medium-high heat. Add chicken fillets and as many breasts as will fit; brown on both sides. Remove from pan. Add remaining breasts and whole mushrooms and brown on both sides. Return first batch of breasts (but not fillets) to pan; then add ginger, sherry, broth, soy, sugar, and vinegar. Cover, reduce heat, and simmer for 7 minutes. Carefully turn breasts over and add fillets. Cover and simmer until breasts are no longer pink when slashed in thickest part (about 3 more minutes). With a slotted spoon, lift out chicken and mushrooms and transfer to a serving dish; keep warm.

Stir cornstarch mixture into pan juices. Increase heat to high and bring liquid to a boil, stirring; then add any juices that have collected on serving dish. If sauce is too thick, thin by stirring in a few drops of water. Spoon sauce over chicken and mushrooms. Makes 6 servings.

Sautéed mushrooms. Insert metal blade. Finely chop ½ pound **fresh shiitake or regular mushrooms** as directed on page 13; set aside. Following directions on same page, mince 1 clove **garlic,** then 1 quarter-size slice **fresh ginger;** leave in work bowl. Finely chop 1 medium-size **onion** as directed on page 13.

Melt 2 tablespoons **butter** or margarine in a wide frying pan over medium heat. Add onion, ginger, garlic, and mushrooms; cook, stirring, until onion is very soft and all liquid has evaporated. Add 1 teaspoon **soy sauce.**

Minced Chicken in Lettuce

∮ To eat this Chinese-style treat, spoon the chicken mixture into a crisp lettuce leaf, fold to enclose, and eat the tasty packet out of hand. Fresh fruit, fortune cookies, and hot tea complete the menu.

  2 large cloves garlic
  1 quarter-size slice fresh ginger
  1 can (8 oz.) sliced bamboo shoots, drained well
  1 can (8 oz.) water chestnuts, drained well
  5 green onions (white part only, cut into 1-inch lengths)
  ¼ pound mushrooms
  1½ pounds chicken breasts (at refrigerator temperature), skinned, boned, split, and cut into chunks
     Cooking sauce (recipe follows)
  4 tablespoons salad oil
  ¼ to ½ teaspoon crushed red pepper
  ½ cup frozen peas, thawed
     Hoisin sauce
     Chilled romaine or butter lettuce leaves

Insert metal blade. Mince garlic, then ginger as directed on page 13; set aside. Place bamboo shoots, water chestnuts, and onions in work bowl. Process, using on-off pulses, until finely chopped; set aside. Chop mushrooms as directed on page 13 and set aside. Chop chicken, half at a time (or all at once in a large-capacity processor), as directed for cooked chicken on page 10. Prepare cooking sauce; set aside.

Heat a wok or 12-inch frying pan over high heat. When pan is hot, add 2 tablespoons of the oil; then add garlic, ginger, and pepper and stir once. Add chicken and stir-fry until opaque (about 3 minutes); remove from pan and set aside.

Add remaining 2 tablespoons oil to pan. When oil is hot, add mushrooms, onions, water chestnuts, and bamboo shoots; stir-fry for 2 minutes. Return chicken to pan and add peas. Stir cooking sauce, pour into pan, and cook, stirring, until sauce boils and thickens. Serve at once.

To eat, spread a little hoisin on a lettuce leaf; spoon on some of the chicken mixture, then wrap up and eat out of hand. Makes 4 to 6 servings.

Cooking sauce. Combine 2 teaspoons **corn-starch,** 1 tablespoon **dry sherry,** 2 tablespoons *each* **soy sauce** and **water,** and ½ teaspoon **sugar.**

Stir-fried Chicken with Cheese

Tangy blue cheese lends unusual flavor to this quick-to-fix entrée. Season the stir-fry with wasabi paste, if you like, but watch out—it's *hot.* (You'll find wasabi paste in Asian markets and well-stocked supermarkets.)

- 1 **large whole chicken breast (about 1 lb.), skinned, boned, split, and frozen until firm**
- 1 **medium-size onion**
- 1 **medium-size red bell pepper, seeded**
- 2 **tablespoons salad oil**
- ½ **cup raw peanuts or unsalted dry-roasted peanuts**
- 2 **cups bean sprouts**
- ½ **to 1 cup (2 to 4 oz.) coarsely crumbled blue-veined cheese**
  Soy sauce
  Wasabi paste or prepared horseradish (optional)

Insert slicing disc. Partially thaw chicken until it passes the knife test (see page 9); then slice as directed on page 10. Set aside. Following directions on pages 13 and 15, slice onion, then bell pepper.

Heat a wok or 12-inch frying pan over high heat. When pan is hot, add 1 tablespoon of the oil; then add peanuts and cook, stirring, until lightly toasted. Lift out and set aside. Add remaining 1 tablespoon oil to pan. When oil is hot, add chicken and stir-fry until opaque throughout (2 to 3 minutes). Lift out and set aside.

Add bell pepper and onion to pan; stir-fry until onion is slightly soft (about 2 minutes). Add

bean sprouts, peanuts, and chicken; stir until heated through. Pour into a serving dish and gently mix in cheese. Pass soy and wasabi (if desired) at the table. Makes 2 or 3 servings.

Turkey Chili

We've used ground turkey along with beans and spices in this fun and festive meal-in-a-bowl. It's somewhat leaner than chilis based on red meat, but just as thick and hearty. Diners add their choice of garnishes at the table.

- 2 **cloves garlic**
- 1 **large onion**
- 1 **small green bell pepper, seeded**
- 1 **can (about 1 lb.) tomatoes, drained (reserve liquid)**
- 3 **tablespoons salad oil**
- 2 **pounds ground turkey**
- 3 **cans (15 oz.** *each***) kidney beans, drained well**
- 2 **cans (15 oz.** *each***) tomato sauce**
- ¼ **cup soy sauce**
- 3 **tablespoons chili powder**
- 1 **teaspoon** *each* **ground cumin, sage leaves, and thyme leaves**
  Garnishes (suggestions follow)

Insert metal blade. Mince garlic as directed on page 13; leave in work bowl. Chop onion as directed on page 13; set onion and garlic aside. Chop bell pepper as directed on page 15 and set aside. Place drained tomatoes in work bowl. Process, using on-off pulses, until chopped.

Heat oil in a 6 to 8-quart kettle over medium-high heat. Add bell pepper, onion, and garlic and cook, stirring, until onion is soft.

Crumble turkey into kettle. Increase heat to high and cook, stirring gently, until meat begins to brown. Add tomatoes and their liquid, beans, tomato sauce, soy, chili powder, cumin, sage, and thyme. Stir, scraping kettle to free browned bits. Cover, reduce heat, and simmer until chili is thick and flavors are well blended (about 30 minutes).

To serve, ladle hot chili into bowls; offer garnishes at the table. Makes 6 to 8 servings.

Garnishes. Offer **lime wedges,** sliced **green onions** (see page 13), shredded **jack or Cheddar cheese** (see page 8), and/or chopped **tomatoes** (see page 15).

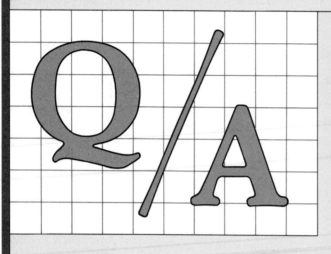

What if cake batter spills over the top of the work bowl? What if chopped onions turn out minced? Here are some common processing problems and ways to avoid them.

Chopped food is uneven. For best results, start with food cut into equal-size pieces (usually 1 to 1½-inch chunks) and fill the work bowl no more than halfway. Use on-off pulses to "stir" food as you chop.

Chopped food turns out minced. You may have processed continuously instead of using on-off pulses. As you process, stop frequently to check consistency before chopping food into smaller pieces.

Chopped food is watery. Foods with a high water content, such as bell peppers and onions, usually give off some liquid when chopped in the processor. But if they turn out very watery, you've overprocessed them; discard them and start over.

Purées aren't smooth. For the smoothest purées, cook foods until very tender, and purée solid food with just enough added liquid to keep it moving in the work bowl. For more puréeing tips, see page 46.

Liquid spills out top of work bowl. When mixing batters or puréeing soups, process only 2 cups at a time in a standard-size work bowl. If you try to process more, liquid will spill over the top. (Large-capacity work bowls can handle more; check manufacturer's instructions.) For more on puréeing, see page 46.

Food is left on top of disc. After processing, a piece or two of food often remains on top of the disc. If you're shredding, stop the machine, take off the cover, and remove food. Then replace the cover, start the machine, and drop food through the feed tube onto the shredding disc. Food usually shreds completely; if it doesn't, repeat the process.

If you're slicing, remove cover and position the remaining piece directly beneath the feed tube. Replace cover, reload feed tube and continue to slice. (If no more food remains to be sliced, remove the leftover piece and slice it by hand.)

Cheese forms balls on shredding disc. Be sure to shred firm and semisoft cheeses directly from the refrigerator to minimize build-up on the disc. (Mozzarella and other semisoft cheeses will leave a few balls on the shredding disc even when processed cold.) Hard cheeses such as Parmesan shouldn't be shredded unless you have a special disc specifically for that purpose.

Slices are uneven. It's normal to have a few uneven slices. If *all* the slices are uneven, you may not have packed the feed tube tightly enough, or you may have used uneven pressure with the pusher. Refer to page 37 for more details on slicing techniques.

Blade falls out when emptying work bowl. Check the bottom of your work bowl—if there's a hole, place one finger in it when emptying the work bowl. The blade won't fall out, even when the bowl is tipped upside down. If a work bowl doesn't have a hole in the bottom, press down on top of the blade (the plastic part) with one hand and tip bowl to empty as much as possible. Then remove blade; scrape food from blade and work bowl. (For stiff mixtures, always remove blade before emptying.)

Enchiladas with Tomatillo Sauce

⊛ ♭ ☺ Green chiles, lime juice, and tart tomatillos give refreshing character to the sauce for these make-ahead chicken enchiladas.

> 1 pound jack cheese
> Chicken filling (recipe follows)
> Tomatillo sauce (recipe follows)
> Salad oil
> 12 corn tortillas (each 6 to 7 inches in diameter)
> Toppings (suggestions follow)

Insert shredding disc. Shred cheese as directed on page 8; set aside. Prepare filling and sauce.

Into a small frying pan, pour oil to a depth of ½ inch; heat over medium-high heat until oil ripples when pan is tilted. Add one tortilla and cook just until it begins to brown (about 5 seconds per side). Lift out and lay flat on paper towels. Spoon about ½ cup of the filling down center of hot tortilla and roll to enclose. Place filled tortilla, seam side down, on a 10 by 15-inch rimmed baking sheet. Repeat with remaining tortillas and filling. (At this point, you may cover enchiladas with foil and refrigerate until next day.)

Bake enchiladas, covered, in a 350° oven until hot throughout (about 15 minutes; about 30 minutes if refrigerated). Uncover and sprinkle with 2 cups of the cheese. Bake, uncovered, until cheese is melted (about 10 more minutes).

While enchiladas bake, prepare toppings. To serve, spoon about ¾ cup sauce onto each of 6 warmed dinner plates; set 2 enchiladas atop sauce on each plate. Pass toppings at the table. Makes 6 servings.

Chicken filling. Insert metal blade. Chop 2 whole **chicken breasts** (cooked, skinned, boned, and cut into chunks) as directed on page 10. Transfer to a mixing bowl; add 2 cups of the shredded **jack cheese,** 1 can (7 oz.) **diced green chiles,** 1½ teaspoons **oregano leaves,** and **salt** to taste.

Tomatillo sauce. Insert metal blade. Chop 2 medium-size **onions** as directed on page 13. Heat 6 tablespoons **salad oil** in a 3 to 4-quart pan over medium-high heat. Add onions and cook, stirring, until soft (about 5 minutes). Stir in 1 can (7 oz.) **diced green chiles,** 2 cans (13 oz. each) **tomatillos** (drained well), 1 cup **regular-strength chicken broth,** 3 tablespoons **lime juice,** 2 teaspoons each **oregano leaves** and **sugar,** and 1 teaspoon **ground cumin.** Reduce heat to low and simmer, uncovered, for 25 minutes to blend flavors. Season to taste with **salt.** Pour into work bowl, a portion at a time (or all at once in a large-capacity processor); process continuously until puréed. If made ahead, cover and refrigerate until next day. Reheat before serving.

Toppings. Insert slicing disc. Shred ½ head **iceberg lettuce** as directed on page 13; place in a bowl. Also offer **lime slices** (see page 9), **sour cream, fresh cilantro** (coriander), **guacamole,** and grated **Parmesan cheese** (see page 8).

Chicken & Vegetable Bundles

☺ Tender strips of pounded chicken breast are wrapped around strips of carrot and zucchini, then skewered for easy cooking.

> 2 whole chicken breasts, skinned, boned, and split
> 1 large carrot (1 to 1½ inches in diameter)
> 2 medium-size zucchini
> 3 tablespoons olive oil or salad oil
> 3 tablespoons lemon juice
> ¼ teaspoon each dry rosemary and salt
> Dash of pepper

Pound each chicken breast half between sheets of plastic wrap until ¼ inch thick; then cut each in half lengthwise.

Insert slicing disc. Cut carrot into julienne strips as directed on page 12; arrange on a rack and steam, covered, over boiling water until tender-crisp to bite (about 5 minutes). Cut zucchini into julienne strips as directed on page 15.

To form bundles, wrap one piece of meat around 3 strips each of carrot and zucchini. For easier handling on the grill, run 2 parallel skewers through each bundle (one through each end, perpendicular to vegetables); thread 2 bundles on each pair of skewers.

Stir together oil, lemon juice, rosemary, salt, and pepper. Place bundles on a greased grill 4 to 6 inches above a solid bed of glowing coals. Cook, turning and brushing with oil mixture, until chicken is opaque throughout when slashed—4 to 5 minutes per side. (Or broil 4 inches below heat.) Makes 4 servings.

Cioppino

𝕊 Cioppino is a cross between a soup and a stew, a hearty dish that's ideal for informal entertaining. It's quick to prepare, because the various shellfish cook in their shells. For the same reason, it's messy to eat—you have to pick the shellfish up with your fingers. Be sure to provide your guests with big napkins, and offer plenty of French bread to soak up the delicious sauce.

    1 medium-size onion
    1 large green bell pepper, seeded
    ½ pound Swiss chard
    2 cloves garlic
    ½ cup lightly packed parsley sprigs
    1½ teaspoons *each* dry basil and marjoram leaves
    ¾ teaspoon *each* dry rosemary, sage leaves, and thyme leaves
   18 small hard-shell clams, scrubbed well
    1 large cooked crab, cleaned and cracked
    1 pound medium-size (30 to 40 per lb.) raw shrimp
    1 pound sea bass, rockfish, or other firm-fleshed white fish fillets, cut into 1-inch strips
    1 large can (28 oz.) tomatoes
    1 can (6 oz.) tomato paste
    ¼ cup olive oil or salad oil
    1 teaspoon salt
    ½ teaspoon freshly ground pepper
    ½ cup dry white wine

Insert metal blade. Following directions on pages 13 and 15, chop onion and transfer to a bowl; then chop bell pepper and add to bowl. Cut chard stems crosswise in 2-inch lengths; cut leaves crosswise in 2-inch strips. Process stems and leaves separately, using on-off pulses, until coarsely chopped; transfer both to bowl with onion and bell pepper.

Mince garlic as directed on page 13; leave in work bowl. Add parsley, basil, marjoram, rosemary, sage, and thyme to work bowl; process, using on-off pulses, until parsley is finely chopped. Add to vegetables in bowl; mix well.

Arrange clams in bottom of a heavy 8-quart kettle. Sprinkle with a third of the vegetable mixture. Layer crab pieces on top; sprinkle with half the remaining vegetable mixture. Rinse shrimp well and arrange atop crab and vegetables; sprinkle with remaining vegetable mixture. Arrange fish on top.

Drain tomatoes, reserving liquid. Place drained tomatoes in work bowl and process, using on-off pulses, until chopped. In a bowl, stir together chopped tomatoes, reserved liquid, tomato paste, oil, salt, and pepper; pour over fish. Cover kettle and bring cioppino to a boil over high heat; then reduce heat to medium-low and simmer for 30 minutes. Pour in wine and simmer for 10 more minutes. Ladle into wide, shallow soup bowls. Makes 6 servings.

Calico Stuffed Trout

𝕊 Chopped vegetable "confetti" makes a fresh and colorful stuffing for whole trout. Each plump little fish is wrapped in a foil packet, then barbecued. Cook them on your back-yard grill, or pack the wrapped fish in a cooler and barbecue at a campground.

    6 whole trout (¾ to 1 lb. *each*), pan dressed
    1 clove garlic, cut in half
    1 small carrot, cut into 1-inch chunks
    ½ small onion
    1 small red or green bell pepper, seeded
    1 small inner stalk celery
    2 tablespoons *each* dry white wine and white wine vinegar
    ½ teaspoon *each* dry basil, oregano leaves, and salt
    ¼ teaspoon pepper
    ⅓ cup salad oil
      Lemon wedges

Rinse trout and pat dry, then rub cut sides of garlic over inside cavity of each. Discard garlic. Cut six 8 by 12-inch pieces of heavy-duty foil; grease foil and center one trout on each piece. Set aside.

Insert metal blade. Place carrot in work bowl and process, using on-off pulses, until chopped; set aside. Following directions on pages 13, 15, and 12, chop onion, then bell pepper, then celery, adding each to carrot after it's chopped.

Place wine, vinegar, basil, oregano, salt, and pepper in work bowl. With motor running, pour oil through feed tube. Continue processing until incorporated.

Evenly spoon vegetable mixture into cavity of each trout; drizzle vegetables with oil mixture. Bring long sides of foil together over trout; fold down to trout. Fold ends of each packet to seal.

Place wrapped trout on a grill 4 to 6 inches above a solid bed of glowing coals. Cook just until fish looks opaque in center (8 to 10 minutes per side—open foil and cut a gash to test). Serve with lemon wedges to squeeze over individual servings. Makes 6 servings.

Shrimp in Mint Beurre Blanc

⌀ The cool flavor of mint combines deliciously with savory shrimp in this light, fresh-tasting entrée. Start by making a mint-flavored butter; then briefly sauté shrimp and stir the flavored butter into the pan juices to make a sauce. Round out the meal with a green salad and crusty French bread or rolls.

Mint butter (recipe follows)
2 to 4 tablespoons butter or margarine
1 to 1½ pounds medium-size raw shrimp (30 to 40 per lb.), shelled and deveined
1 cup dry white wine
Lemon slices (see page 9) and fresh mint sprigs

Prepare mint butter and set aside.

Melt 2 tablespoons of the (unflavored) butter in a wide frying pan over medium heat. Add shrimp and cook, stirring, until pink (about 5 minutes). Lift out shrimp with a slotted spoon; keep warm.

Add wine to pan, increase heat to high, and bring to a boil. Boil, stirring occasionally, until reduced to about ⅓ cup. Reduce heat to low or remove pan from heat. Add mint butter all at once, stirring constantly to blend in butter as it melts. For a thicker sauce, add 2 more tablespoons (unflavored) butter, all at once; stir constantly until combined. Pour sauce onto a rimmed platter and arrange shrimp on top. Garnish with lemon slices and mint sprigs. Serve immediately. Makes 4 servings.

Mint butter. Insert metal blade. Cut four ½ by 1-inch strips of **lemon zest** (colored outer layer of peel); also cut ¼ cup **butter** or margarine into 4 chunks.

With motor running, drop butter chunks and zest strips alternately through feed tube. Stop motor. Add 1 cup lightly packed **fresh mint leaves** to work bowl. Process continuously (stop-ping to scrape bowl once or twice) until smooth and well blended. If made ahead, cover and refrigerate until next day.

Salmon Steaks with Fish Mousse

⌀ Golden puffs of sole mousse top salmon steaks in this elegant company dish. You pour white wine into the baking pan, so the fish "poaches" gently and turns out moist and tender. Offer asparagus and tiny thin-skinned potatoes alongside the succulent steaks.

1 small shallot or 1 green onion (white part only, cut into 1-inch lengths)
½ pound sole or lingcod fillets
1 egg
½ cup whipping cream
Salt and white pepper
4 salmon steaks, *each* about 1 inch thick
1 cup dry white wine
½ teaspoon thyme leaves
¼ cup butter or margarine

Insert metal blade. Chop shallot as directed on page 15; set aside.

Pull any bones from sole with pliers or tweezers, then cut fish into chunks. Place fish in work bowl and process continuously until puréed. Add egg and ¼ cup of the cream to work bowl; process continuously until combined. Season to taste with salt and pepper.

Arrange salmon steaks side by side in a 9 by 13-inch baking dish. Evenly top steaks with sole mixture, then carefully pour wine around them. Bake, uncovered, in a 450° oven just until mousse topping is lightly browned and salmon steaks look opaque in center (15 to 20 minutes—cut a gash to test).

With a slotted spatula, transfer steaks to a platter; keep warm. Pour cooking liquid through a wire strainer into a wide frying pan. Add remaining ¼ cup cream, thyme, and shallot; bring to a boil over high heat, then boil rapidly until reduced to ½ cup.

Reduce heat to low. Add butter all at once, stirring constantly to incorporate butter as it melts. Season to taste with salt and pepper. Spoon sauce over and around steaks. Makes 4 servings.

Salmon Quenelles

(Pictured on facing page)

Delicate quenelles are one of the glories of classic French cuisine. Fortunately, though, you need no longer prepare these light fish "dumplings" the traditional way; with the processor's help, a mixture that once took hours to assemble goes together in seconds. Our quenelles are made with salmon and served on a pool of basil sauce. Try the scallop variation with Pimento Beurre Blanc (page 67) or Tarragon-saffron sauce.

- 1 **pound salmon fillet, skinned and cut into chunks**
- 2 **egg whites**
- ⅔ **cup very cold whipping cream**
- 1 **tablespoon chopped fresh chives**
  Salt and white pepper
  Basil sauce (recipe follows)
  Fresh basil sprigs

Insert metal blade. Place salmon chunks and egg whites in work bowl. With motor running, slowly pour cream through feed tube; continue processing until mixture is smooth and well blended. Add chives, then season to taste with salt and pepper. Process just to combine. (At this point, you may transfer mixture to a mixing bowl, then cover and refrigerate for up to 24 hours.)

Prepare as much of basil sauce as can be done ahead.

To cook quenelles, bring 2 inches of salted water to a boil in a deep 10 to 12-inch frying pan over high heat. Reduce heat to keep water at a simmer. Place a large plate in a 200° oven to warm.

Use 2 moistened soup spoons to shape quenelles. Scoop out about 2 tablespoons of the salmon mixture with one spoon; with second spoon, smooth top of mixture to make a smooth egg shape. Then use second spoon to ease mixture off first spoon into simmering water.

Repeat to make more quenelles (you can cook about 4 at a time). Poach, uncovered, until quenelles float to the surface and feel firm when lightly pressed (2 to 3 minutes). Transfer with a slotted spoon to warmed plate; return plate to oven while cooking remaining quenelles.

Finish preparing basil sauce. Spoon sauce evenly onto heated dinner plates. Arrange 3 or 4 quenelles on each plate; garnish each serving with a basil sprig. Makes about 6 servings.

Basil sauce. Insert metal blade. Mince 1 **green onion** (white part only, cut into 1-inch lengths), as directed on page 15; set aside. Chop 3 large **mushrooms** as directed on page 13; set aside. Melt 2 tablespoons **butter** or margarine in a wide frying pan over medium-high heat. Add onion and cook, stirring, until soft. Stir in mushrooms, 3 tablespoons **dry white wine,** 1 tablespoon **dry sherry,** and ½ cup **regular-strength chicken broth.** Cook, uncovered, stirring occasionally, until reduced to ½ cup. Remove from heat.

Meanwhile, place 3 cups lightly packed **fresh basil leaves** in work bowl. Process, using on-off pulses, until finely chopped. With motor running, pour mushroom mixture through feed tube; continue processing (stopping to scrape bowl once) until sauce is smooth and well combined. Return sauce to pan. (At this point, you may cover sauce and let stand at room temperature for up to 6 hours.

Just before serving, add 1¼ cups **whipping cream** to pan. Bring to a boil over high heat. Reduce heat and add ½ cup (¼ lb.) **butter** or margarine all at once; stirring constantly to blend in butter as it melts. If desired, pour sauce through a fine wire strainer before serving.

Scallop Quenelles

Insert metal blade. Follow directions for **Salmon Quenelles** (this page) but substitute 1 pound **scallops** (rinsed and patted dry) for salmon. Serve with **Tarragon-saffron sauce** (recipe follows) instead of basil sauce. Garnish each serving with a **fresh tarragon sprig,** if desired.

Tarragon-saffron sauce. Insert metal blade. Mince 1 small **shallot** as directed on page 15. Melt 1 tablespoon **butter** or margarine in a wide frying pan over medium-high heat. Stir in 1 tablespoon finely chopped **fresh tarragon** or ½ teaspoon dry tarragon. Add ¾ cup **dry white wine,** 1½ cups **regular-strength chicken broth,** and 1/32 teaspoon **ground saffron.**

Bring mixture to a boil over high heat and continue to boil, uncovered, until reduced by half. Add ½ cup **whipping cream** and boil rapidly until reduced to about 1 cup. (At this point, you may cover sauce and let stand at room temperature for up to 6 hours; reheat before continuing.)

Reduce heat to low and add ½ cup (¼ lb.) **butter** or margarine all at once; stir constantly to incorporate butter as it melts.

Salmon Quenelles

1 Pour refrigerator-temperature whipping cream through feed tube while salmon and egg whites whirl in work bowl.

2 Add chopped chives after cream is incorporated, so they'll stay in distinct pieces.

3 To shape quenelles, scoop out about 2 tablespoons of the salmon mixture with a moistened soup spoon. Then use the back of a second moistened soup spoon to smooth top and sides.

4 Gently slide each quenelle into simmering water, using second spoon to ease quenelle off spoon it's resting on.

Pasta, Pizza & Breads

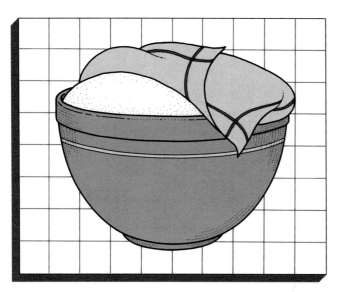

Spring Harvest Pasta Salad

Whimsical corkscrew-shaped pasta (called *rotelle* in Italian) holds onto all the piquant mustard vinaigrette in this sprightly salad.

- ¼ **pound green beans, ends removed**
- ¾ **pound broccoli, tough stem ends removed**
- 8 **medium-size mushrooms**
- 8 **ounces rotelle or other pasta twists**
  Boiling salted water
  Mustard vinaigrette (recipe follows)
  Salt

Insert slicing disc. French-cut green beans as directed on page 12. Arrange beans on a rack and steam, covered, over boiling water until tender-crisp to bite (about 30 seconds). Plunge into cold water to cover; when cool, drain well.

Cut flowerets from broccoli. Peel stems; cut into lengths to fit vertically in feed tube, then pack into tube and slice. Place sliced stems and flowerets on rack over boiling water; steam, covered, until tender-crisp to bite (about 2 minutes). Plunge into cold water to cover; when cool, drain well.

Slice mushrooms as directed on page 13. Cover and refrigerate mushrooms, broccoli, and beans.

Following package directions, cook pasta in boiling salted water until *al dente*; drain well. Prepare mustard vinaigrette.

In a large bowl, combine pasta and vinaigrette; mix well and season to taste with salt. Cover and refrigerate for at least 6 hours or until next day, stirring often.

Add mushrooms, broccoli, and beans to pasta; mix well. Serve at once, or cover and let stand at room temperature for up to 4 hours. Makes 4 to 6 servings.

Mustard vinaigrette. Insert metal blade. Chop 1 cup lightly packed **parsley sprigs** as directed on page 15; leave in work bowl. Chop ½ small **red onion** as directed on page 13. Place onion and parsley in a mixing bowl with 2 tablespoons **Dijon mustard,** ⅓ cup **white wine vinegar,** and 1 cup **olive oil** or salad oil. Stir well.

Rigatoni with Kielbasa & Zucchini

This skillet supper is ideal for a busy night; you can prepare the ingredients in no time, and cooking takes just minutes.

- 1½ **cups rigatoni**
  Boiling salted water
- 1 **medium-size red onion**
- 3 **small zucchini**
- 2 **kielbasa (Polish sausages), about ¾ pound** *total*
  Dijon herb sauce (recipe follows)

In a wide frying pan, cook rigatoni in 1 inch of boiling salted water until *al dente* (10 to 15 minutes). Drain well and set aside. While pasta cooks, insert slicing disc. Following directions on pages 13 and 15, slice onion, then zucchini, setting each aside separately. Slice sausages as directed on page 10. Prepare Dijon herb sauce; set aside.

Rinse and dry pan and place over medium-high heat. Add sausages and cook, stirring, for 1 minute. Add onion and cook, stirring, until soft (about 3 more minutes). Stir in zucchini and cook, stirring, just until tender-crisp to bite (about 2 more minutes). Add rigatoni and Dijon herb sauce; cook and stir until mixture is hot throughout (1 to 2 more minutes). Makes 3 or 4 servings.

Dijon herb sauce. In a small bowl, combine 3 tablespoons **red wine vinegar** and 1 tablespoon *each* **Dijon mustard** and **dry basil.**

Cheese & Mushroom Manicotti

Big pasta shells stuffed with cheeses and fresh vegetables make a hearty meatless entrée or a satisfying side dish. There's no need to precook the manicotti; they absorb moisture from the sauce as they bake.

- 1 **sandwich-size slice firm-textured fresh bread**
- ¼ **cup lightly packed parsley sprigs**
- ½ **small onion, cut into chunks**
- 1 **small stalk celery, cut into chunks**
- ¼ **pound mushrooms**
- 8 **ounces** *each* **mozzarella cheese and sharp Cheddar cheese**
- 1 **can (2¼ oz.) sliced ripe olives, drained well**
- ¼ **teaspoon pepper**
- 1 **egg, lightly beaten**
- ¼ **cup milk**
- 4 **cups marinara sauce, purchased or homemade (page 108)**
- 1 **cup water**
- 2 **packages (3¾ oz.** *each***) manicotti shells**
  Grated Parmesan cheese (see page 8)

Insert metal blade. Process bread into crumbs as directed on page 10; transfer to a large mixing bowl. Place parsley, onion, and celery in work bowl. Process, using on-off pulses, until chopped. Add to bread crumbs. Chop mushrooms as directed on page 13; add to bread crumb mixture.

Change to shredding disc. Following directions on page 8, shred mozzarella cheese and set aside; then shred Cheddar cheese. Add half the mozzarella and all the Cheddar to bread crumb mixture; then add olives, pepper, egg, and milk. Stir to mix thoroughly and set aside.

Stir together marinara sauce and water; pour about 2½ cups into a 9 by 13-inch baking pan.

Stuff manicotti shells with cheese mixture, placing stuffed shells on sauce in pan. Pour remaining sauce over top, cover pan with foil, and bake in a 375° oven for 1 hour. Remove foil, sprinkle remaining mozzarella over top, and bake until pasta shells are tender when pierced and cheese is melted (about 10 more minutes). Pass Parmesan at the table. Makes 6 to 8 servings.

Homemade Pasta with Pesto (Recipe_on page 107)

1 Making noodles is simple: Process flour, salt, and eggs, then pour water through feed tube while motor is running.

2 Dough in bowl at top left is dry and crumbly; it needs more water. Bottom bowl of dough is wet and sticky; it needs more flour. Bowl of dough at right is moist and pliant, but not overly sticky.

3 To roll dough by machine, feed it through rollers (flour it if it's sticky). Repeat, setting rollers closer together each time, until dough is as thin as you like.

4 Let rolled-out strips dry until they feel like a chamois cloth (5 to 10 minutes); then feed strips through cutting blade. Wide blade makes fettuccine.

Fresh Egg Noodles

(Pictured on facing page)

Making fresh pasta at home is a snap in a processor; it mixes and kneads the dough for you in seconds. And once you've tasted the results, packaged pasta will be a thing of the past.

About 2 cups all-purpose flour
2 **eggs**
½ **teaspoon salt**
About ¼ cup water
4 **quarts boiling salted water**
Butter, salt, and pepper

Insert metal blade. Place 2 cups of the flour, eggs, and salt in work bowl; process continuously until mixture resembles cornmeal. With motor running, pour ¼ cup of the water through feed tube and continue processing until dough forms a ball. Stop machine. Dough should be well blended, but not sticky. If dough feels sticky, add flour, 1 tablespoon at a time, processing after each addition. If dough looks crumbly, add water, 1 teaspoon at a time, processing after each addition.

Roll and cut dough as directed below. If you plan to use a pasta machine, you can roll dough immediately. If you plan to use a rolling pin, cover dough and let it rest for 20 minutes.

Once noodles are cut, it's best to cook them right away. But if you make more noodles than you need, you can let them stand, uncovered, until they're dry but still pliable (30 minutes to 1 hour). Then place them in a plastic bag and refrigerate for up to 2 days.

To cook noodles, drop them into boiling salted water and cook until *al dente* (1 to 2 minutes). Pour into a colander; drain well. Season to taste with butter, salt, and pepper (or top with a sauce); serve at once. Makes about 4 cups noodles.

Rolling & cutting by machine. The following general directions apply to both manual and electric pasta machines.

Rolling. Flatten a fourth of the dough slightly; flour it, then feed it through the widest roller setting. Fold dough into thirds and feed through rollers again. Repeat folding and rolling 8 to 10 times or until dough is elastic. If dough feels damp or sticky, flour both sides each time it's rolled.

When dough is smooth and pliable, set rollers one notch closer together and feed dough through. Flour dough if it's damp or sticky. Repeat rolling, setting rollers closer each time, until dough is a long strip of the desired thickness.

Cut strip in half crosswise for easy handling; place on a floured surface or cloth and leave uncovered while you roll remaining portions. Let each strip dry until it feels leathery but still pliable, like a chamois cloth (5 to 10 minutes).

Cutting. Feed each strip through medium-wide blades for fettuccine or through narrow blades for thin noodles (tagliarini). Lightly flour cut noodles to keep strands separate. Once cut, noodles can be handled in 2 ways: you can toss them in a loose pile, or you can carefully gather strands as they emerge from machine and lay them in neat rows.

Rolling & cutting by hand. If you're rolling pasta by hand, be sure to let the dough rest for 20 minutes after kneading in the food processor. This resting time reduces the dough's elasticity, making it easier to roll.

Rolling. On a lightly floured board, roll out a fourth of the dough to a rectangle about 1/16 inch thick. If dough is damp or sticky, turn and flour both sides as you roll. Transfer rolled strip to a lightly floured surface or cloth and leave uncovered while you roll out remaining portions. Let each strip dry until it feels leathery but still pliable, like a chamois cloth (5 to 10 minutes).

Cutting. Place a strip of rolled pasta dough on a lightly floured board and sprinkle with flour. Starting at narrow end, roll up jelly roll style and cut into slices as wide as you want the noodle. Fettuccine is usually about ¼ inch wide, tagliarini about ⅛ inch; lasagne is about 2 inches wide.

Fresh Spinach Noodles

Cook half of 1 package (10 oz.) **frozen chopped spinach** according to package directions; pour into a colander and let cool, then squeeze out as much liquid as possible. (Or use ½ cup very well drained cooked fresh spinach.) Place spinach in work bowl with 2 **eggs** and process continuously until spinach is finely chopped. Add 2 cups **all-purpose flour** and ½ teaspoon **salt;** process continuously until dough forms a ball. If necessary, add water or more flour, following directions for **Fresh Egg Noodles.** If rolling by hand, cover and let rest for 20 minutes. Roll, cut, and cook as directed for **Fresh Egg Noodles.** Makes about 4 cups noodles.

Rotolo Italiano

Despite its dramatic appearance, a *rotolo* is easy to prepare. You just roll pasta dough into a thin rectangle, then wrap it jelly roll style around a savory spinach filling.

⅓ **cup pine nuts**
Spinach filling (recipe follows)
Tomato cream sauce (recipe follows)
About 1⅓ cups all-purpose flour
2 **eggs**
2 **tablespoons olive oil or salad oil**
Grated Parmesan cheese (see page 8)

Spread pine nuts in a shallow baking pan and toast in a 350° oven until golden (about 8 minutes). Set aside. Prepare spinach filling and tomato cream sauce; set both aside.

Insert metal blade. Place 1 cup of the flour in work bowl. In a measuring cup, stir together eggs and oil. With motor running, pour mixture through feed tube and continue processing until dough holds together. Add up to ⅓ cup more flour, 1 tablespoon at a time, processing after each addition, until dough forms a nonsticky ball. Cover dough and let rest for at least 5 minutes.

On a floured board, roll out dough to a 15 by 17-inch rectangle; flour board frequently to prevent sticking. Trim edges even. Spread filling over rectangle to within 3 inches of long edge farthest from you and to within 1 inch of other edges. Starting from long edge near you, roll up jelly roll style to form a smooth cylinder. Dampen ends and seam with water; press firmly to seal.

To cook the rotolo, you'll need a long pan with a rack (such as a fish poacher) or a kettle at least 10 inches in diameter.

To cook in a long pan, wrap rotolo in cheesecloth; tie string around ends and at several places along roll. Place on pan rack and lower into boiling water to cover. Cook over high heat until boil resumes; cover, reduce heat, and simmer until pasta looks very crinkly (you can see through cheesecloth) and feels firm when pressed with the back of a spoon (20 to 30 minutes).

To cook in a kettle, cut roll in half crosswise; pinch cut ends to seal. Wrap each half in cheesecloth and tie at ends and middle to secure. Place in kettle and add boiling water to cover. Complete cooking as directed above.

Drain most of the water from pan, then lift out roll; let cool for 5 minutes. Snip strings. Gently turn onto a platter, removing cheesecloth; join halves together, if necessary. If made ahead, place on an ovenproof platter or rimmed baking sheet at least 18 inches long; cover and let stand for up to 3 hours. Then bake, covered, in a 350° oven until hot throughout (25 to 30 minutes).

Spoon hot tomato cream sauce around roll; sprinkle with pine nuts. To serve, cut into 1½-inch slices, spooning sauce alongside. Pass cheese and remaining sauce at the table. Makes 10 servings.

Spinach filling. Discard tough stems from 2¼ pounds **spinach,** then rinse leaves well. Place leaves (with water that clings to them), half at a time, in a wide frying pan; cover and cook over medium heat until wilted (3 to 5 minutes), stirring once. Pour into a colander. Let cool, then squeeze out as much liquid as possible.

Insert metal blade. Grate 5 ounces **Parmesan cheese** as directed on page 8; set aside. Place spinach in work bowl and process continuously until chopped; set aside. Chop 1 large **onion** as directed on page 13 and set aside. Chop ⅓ pound **mushrooms** as directed on page 13.

Melt ¼ cup **butter** or margarine in a wide frying pan over medium-high heat. Add mushrooms and onion and cook, stirring, until onion is soft and liquid has evaporated. Remove from heat; beat in spinach, Parmesan cheese, ¼ cup (about 1 oz.) chopped **prosciutto** or cooked ham, 2 cups **ricotta cheese,** 2 **eggs,** and ¼ teaspoon *each* **ground nutmeg** and **pepper.** If made ahead, cover and refrigerate until next day.

Tomato cream sauce. Insert metal blade. Place 1 large **carrot** (cut into chunks) in work bowl; process, using on-off pulses, until finely chopped. Set aside. Finely chop 1 small **onion** as directed on page 13.

Melt ½ cup (¼ lb.) **butter** or margarine in a wide frying pan over medium-high heat. Add onion and carrot and cook, stirring, until onion is soft. Add ½ teaspoon **sugar** and 1 large can (28 oz.) **pear-shaped tomatoes** and their liquid; break tomatoes up with a spoon. Simmer, uncovered, until sauce is reduced to 3 cups (about 30 minutes). Pour into work bowl, about half at a time (or all at once in a large-capacity processor); process continuously until puréed. Season to taste with **salt.** (At this point, you may let cool, then cover and refrigerate until next day.) At serving time, combine tomato sauce and ½ cup **whipping cream** in a small pan; bring to a boil over medium-high heat, stirring. Serve hot.

Garden Fettuccine

Colorful vegetables from the garden make a bright, lively sauce for fresh fettuccine. Adapt the recipe to what you have on hand; if green beans or zucchini are in plentiful supply, you might try substituting them for some of the vegetables we suggest here. Make your own noodles from the recipe on page 79, or use purchased fresh or dried fettuccine.

- ½ cup lightly packed parsley sprigs
- 1 clove garlic
- 1 small green bell pepper, seeded
- 3 medium-size tomatoes, peeled, cut into quarters, and seeded
- 4 green onions
- 2 tablespoons olive oil or salad oil
- ½ recipe Fresh Egg Noodles (page 79), 8 to 10 ounces purchased fresh fettuccine, or 4 ounces dried fettuccine
- 3 quarts boiling salted water
- ¼ cup butter or margarine
- ⅔ cup whipping cream
  Salt and pepper
  Grated Parmesan cheese (see page 8)

Insert metal blade. Chop parsley as directed on page 15; set aside. Mince garlic as directed on page 13 and leave in work bowl, then chop bell pepper as directed on page 15. Set both aside. Chop tomatoes as directed on page 15 and set aside.

Change to slicing disc. Slice onions as directed on page 13.

Heat oil in a wide frying pan over medium-high heat. Add garlic and bell pepper and cook, stirring occasionally, until pepper is soft. Add onions and cook, stirring, for 1 to 2 more minutes; then mix in tomatoes and parsley and cook until tomatoes are heated through. Cover and remove from heat.

In a 5 to 6-quart kettle, cook noodles in boiling salted water just until *al dente*—1 to 2 minutes. (Or cook dried noodles according to package directions.) Pour pasta into a colander and drain well. Immediately return kettle to high heat; add butter and cream and boil until butter is melted. Remove kettle from heat and add pasta and vegetables. Mix, lifting and turning with 2 forks. Season to taste with salt and pepper. Pour onto a warm platter and sprinkle generously with cheese. Makes about 6 first-course or side-dish servings.

Green Noodles with Scallops

Green noodles, tender-crisp vegetables, and a delicate cream sauce blend beautifully with thinly sliced scallops. The pasta readily absorbs the distinctive flavor of the succulent shellfish and helps stretch just one pound to serve four to six.

- 2 large carrots
- 2 small red bell peppers, seeded
- 8 green onions
- ½ cup (¼ lb.) butter or margarine
- ⅔ cup dry white wine
- 1 pound scallops, thinly sliced
- 1½ cups whipping cream
- 1 recipe Fresh Spinach Noodles (page 79), about 1 pound purchased fresh spinach noodles, or 8 ounces dried medium-wide spinach noodles
- 4 quarts boiling salted water
  Salt and pepper
  Freshly grated nutmeg

Insert slicing disc. Cut carrots into julienne strips as directed on page 12; set aside. Following directions on pages 15 and 13, slice bell peppers and set aside; then slice onions.

Melt 2 tablespoons of the butter in a wide frying pan over high heat. Add carrots and cook, stirring, until tender-crisp to bite (2 to 3 minutes); set aside. Melt 1 more tablespoon butter in pan; add bell peppers and cook, stirring, until slightly soft (about 1 minute). Set aside. Melt 1 more tablespoon butter in pan. Add onions and cook, stirring, just until heated through. Set aside with peppers and carrots.

Pour wine into pan and bring to a boil. Add scallops, cover, and cook just until scallops are opaque throughout (about 3 minutes—cut a gash to test). With a slotted spoon, lift out scallops; add to vegetables. Add cream to pan and bring to a rolling boil; boil until liquid is reduced to 1¾ cups total. Reduce heat to low; add remaining ¼ cup butter and stir constantly until melted.

Cook fresh noodles in boiling salted water just until *al dente*—1 to 2 minutes. (Or cook dried noodles according to package directions.) Pour noodles into a colander and drain; add to sauce and mix, lifting and turning with 2 forks. Add scallops and vegetables. Season to taste with salt, pepper, and nutmeg. Makes 4 to 6 servings.

Egg Roll Cannelloni

ᗧ Some sources claim that pasta is really an adaptation of Chinese *mein*, discovered by Marco Polo on his travels and brought back to his homeland. We continue the tradition here, using purchased egg roll skins to make Italian cannelloni. The ready-made wrappers speed preparation considerably—and you may even prefer them to homemade pasta, since they're thinner and more delicate.

    Chicken-ham filling (recipe follows)
    Tomato sauce (recipe follows)
12 **egg roll skins**
1 **pound teleme or jack cheese**

Prepare filling and sauce. Mound about ⅓ cup filling along one long edge of each egg roll skin; roll to enclose. Divide half the sauce evenly among 6 individual baking dishes, each about 4 by 6 inches. Place 2 cannelloni in each dish, seam side down and slightly apart. Spread with remaining sauce.

Cut cheese into 12 slices, each just slightly larger than top of each cannelloni; place one slice on each cannelloni. Bake, uncovered, in a 400° oven until hot throughout (30 to 40 minutes). Let stand for about 10 minutes before serving. Makes 6 servings.

Chicken-ham filling. Insert metal blade. Grate 3 ounces **Parmesan cheese** as directed on page 8; set aside. Coarsely chop 6 ounces **cooked ham** or prosciutto as directed on page 10; set aside with cheese. Chop 1 large **onion** as directed on page 13. Melt 2 tablespoons **butter** or margarine in a wide frying pan over medium heat. Add onion and cook, stirring often, until very soft.

Meanwhile, cut 1 pound **chicken breasts** (skinned and boned) into 1½-inch chunks. Add to onion and cook, stirring, until no longer pink when slashed (about 3 minutes). Place chicken and onion in work bowl and process, using on-off pulses, until coarsely chopped. Add 2 **egg yolks,** 1 cup **ricotta cheese,** and ⅛ to ¼ teaspoon **ground nutmeg.** Process, using on-off pulses, just until blended.

Add Parmesan cheese and ham; process, using on-off pulses (stopping to scrape bowl once or twice), just until combined. Season to taste with **salt** and **white pepper.** If made ahead, cover and refrigerate until next day.

Tomato sauce. Prepare a double recipe of **Tomato cream sauce** (page 80), but *don't* double the amount of whipping cream. Instead, use ½ cup *each* whipping cream and **regular-strength chicken broth.**

Mushroom-Pepperoni Pizza

(Pictured on facing page and on front cover)

ᗧ ◔ ▦ Homemade pizza is a processor natural. The processor takes care of everything—it kneads the dough for the chewy crust, shreds the creamy cheese, and does all the chopping and slicing for sauce and toppings.

    Pizza dough (page 84)
2 **cloves garlic**
1 **medium-size onion**
2 **tablespoons olive oil or salad oil**
1 **can (15 oz.) tomato sauce**
1½ **teaspoons dry basil**
1 **teaspoon oregano leaves**
1 **large red or green bell pepper, seeded**
¼ **pound mushrooms**
8 **ounces jack cheese**
    Cornmeal
2 **ounces sliced pepperoni or Italian sausage**

Prepare pizza dough.

While dough is rising, insert metal blade and mince garlic as directed on page 13; leave in work bowl. Chop onion as directed on page 13.

Heat oil in a wide frying pan over medium heat; add onion and garlic and cook, stirring, until onion is soft. Add tomato sauce, basil, and oregano. Bring to a boil; then reduce heat and simmer, uncovered, stirring often, until very thick (12 to 15 minutes). Remove from heat and let cool.

Change to slicing disc. Following directions on pages 15 and 13, slice bell pepper, then mushrooms; set aside. Change to shredding disc. Shred cheese as directed on page 8.

Punch down pizza dough and knead briefly on a lightly floured board. Roll out to a 14-inch circle; lift onto a greased, cornmeal-dusted 14-inch pizza pan. Spread sauce over dough, then arrange pepper slices, mushrooms, and pepperoni on top. Sprinkle evenly with cheese.

Bake pizza on lowest rack in a 400° oven until crust is well browned (20 to 25 minutes). Let stand for 5 minutes, then cut into wedges and serve. Makes 4 to 6 servings.

(Continued on page 84)

Mushroom-Pepperoni Pizza

1 To slice bell peppers, cut in half lengthwise and remove stem and seeds. Place each half, stem end down, in feed tube; slice.

2 To shred cheese, place as large a piece as will fit in feed tube; shred. Use cheese directly from refrigerator.

3 Roll dough out to an even circle about 14 inches in diameter. If dough is stretchy and hard to roll, cover and let rest for a few minutes. Fit rolled dough into a 14-inch pizza pan.

4 Spread spicy tomato sauce evenly over dough circle; then layer peppers, mushrooms, sausage slices, and cheese over all.

Pizza dough. In a measuring cup, dissolve 1 package **active dry yeast** and 1 teaspoon **sugar** in ¾ cup **warm water** (about 110°); let stand until bubbly (about 10 minutes). Stir in 2 tablespoons **olive oil** or salad oil and 1 teaspoon **salt.**

Insert metal blade or plastic dough blade. Place 3 cups **all-purpose flour** in work bowl. With motor running, pour yeast mixture through feed tube in a steady stream, as fast as flour absorbs it. When dough forms a ball, stop machine. Dough should be slightly moist. (If it's too wet, add more flour, 1 tablespoon at a time, processing after each addition.) Process continuously for 45 seconds to knead. Shape dough into a ball. Place in a greased bowl and turn to grease top, then cover and let rise in a warm place until doubled (1 to 1½ hours).

Garlic Cheese Bread

Prepare **Pizza dough** as directed for **Mushroom-Pepperoni Pizza.** While dough is rising, insert metal blade and mince 3 or 4 large cloves **garlic** as directed on page 13. Heat 3 tablespoons **olive oil** or salad oil in a small pan over low heat. Add garlic and cook, stirring occasionally, until soft and yellow (5 to 10 minutes); set aside. Grate 1¼ ounces **Parmesan cheese** as directed on page 8.

Punch down dough and knead briefly on a floured board. Roll dough with a rolling pin, then stretch it with your hands to fit bottom of a well-greased 10 by 15-inch rimmed baking pan. With your fingers or the tip of a spoon, pierce dough (part way through) at 1-inch intervals. Drizzle garlic-oil mixture evenly over dough, then sprinkle with cheese. Let rise, uncovered, in a warm place until puffy (10 to 15 minutes).

Bake in a 400° oven until golden brown (15 to 18 minutes). Cut into 16 equal pieces and serve warm. Makes 16 pieces.

Onion Bread

Prepare **Pizza dough** as directed for **Mushroom-Pepperoni Pizza.** While dough is rising, insert slicing disc. Slice 5 **green onions** as directed on page 13. Fit dough in a 10 by 15-inch pan and pierce as directed for **Garlic Cheese Bread;** brush with 3 tablespoons **olive oil** (do not heat). Sprinkle evenly with 1 teaspoon **coarse salt,** then the sliced onions. Let rise and bake as directed for **Garlic Cheese Bread.**

Pizza Turnovers

What tastes just like pizza, but looks like a giant turnover? Italian *calzone*. Fill these plump, crusty "sandwiches" with spicy sausage or tangy goat cheese, and serve them for lunch or supper.

> **Pizza dough (this page)**
> **Sausage or chèvre filling (recipes follow)**
> **Olive oil or salad oil**
> **Cornmeal**

Prepare Pizza dough. While dough is rising, prepare your choice of filling.

Punch down dough and knead briefly on a lightly floured board; then divide in half for 2 large turnovers, or into quarters for 4 individual turnovers. Shape each portion into a ball; roll large balls into 11-inch circles, small ones into 8½-inch circles. Brush surface of each circle lightly with oil.

Spread half the filling over half of each large dough circle, or a quarter over half of each small circle. Fold plain half over filling, then press edges together. Roll ½ inch of pressed edges up and over; seal and crimp. With a wide spatula, transfer turnovers to greased and cornmeal-dusted baking sheets. Prick tops with a fork and brush lightly with oil. Bake in a 450° oven until well browned (15 to 20 minutes for either size). Serve hot. Makes 4 servings.

Sausage filling. Insert metal blade. Mince 1 clove **garlic** as directed on page 13; leave in work bowl. Change to slicing disc. Following directions on pages 12, 13, and 15, slice 1 small **carrot,** ¼ pound **mushrooms,** 1 small **onion,** and 1 small **green bell pepper.**

Remove casings from 10 ounces (about 3) **mild Italian sausages;** crumble meat into a wide frying pan and cook over medium heat, stirring, until browned. Add sliced vegetables and garlic; cook, stirring, until vegetables are soft. Stir in 1 can (8 oz.) **tomato sauce,** 1 can (2¼ oz.) **sliced ripe olives** (drained well), 1 teaspoon **dry basil,** ½ teaspoon *each* **oregano leaves** and **sugar,** and ¼ teaspoon **crushed red pepper.** Reduce heat and simmer, uncovered, for about 5 minutes. Let cool to room temperature.

Change to metal blade. Grate 2½ ounces **Parmesan cheese** as directed on page 8; leave in work bowl. Change to shredding disc and shred 8 ounces **mozzarella cheese** as directed on page 8. Stir cheeses into cooled filling; season to taste with **salt** and **pepper.**

Chèvre filling. Insert metal blade. Mince 2 cloves **garlic** as directed on page 13; leave in work bowl. Add 12 ounces **mozzarella cheese** (cut into chunks) and process, using on-off pulses, until chopped. Crumble in 6 ounces ripened **chèvre** (such as bûcheron); then add ¼ teaspoon **pepper** and ¼ teaspoon *each* **oregano, marjoram,** and **thyme leaves.** Process, using on-off pulses, until mixture is well combined. Transfer to a mixing bowl. Trim and discard fat from one thick slice (about ¼ lb.) **prosciutto** or cooked ham; cut meat into chunks. Place in work bowl and chop as directed on page 10. Stir into cheese mixture.

Zucchini Nut Tea Bread

When your garden swamps you with zucchini, put some of the crop to use in this moist, spicy tea bread. It's an ideal partner for lunchtime soup or salad, and good all by itself for midnight snacking or breakfast on the run.

    3 cups all-purpose flour
    2 teaspoons ground cinnamon
 1½ teaspoons baking powder
    1 teaspoon baking soda
    ½ teaspoon *each* ground cloves and ground
       nutmeg
    1 cup walnut halves
    2 cups sugar
    1 cup salad oil
    2 teaspoons vanilla
    3 eggs
    ½ pound zucchini

Insert metal blade. Place flour, cinnamon, baking powder, baking soda, cloves, nutmeg, and walnuts in work bowl. Process continuously until walnuts are chopped. Transfer to a large mixing bowl.

Place sugar, oil, and vanilla in work bowl. With motor running, pour eggs through feed tube; continue processing until mixture is well blended. Pour over flour mixture; stir just to blend.

Change to shredding disc. Shred zucchini as directed on page 15. Gently stir into batter just until evenly combined.

Spoon batter into 2 greased 4½ by 8½-inch loaf pans. Bake in a 350° oven until a wooden pick inserted in center comes out clean (about 1 hour and 10 minutes). Let cool in pans on a rack for 10 minutes; then turn loaves out onto rack and let cool right side up.

Serve at once; or wrap airtight and refrigerate for up to 1 week, or freeze for up to 2 months. Makes 2 loaves.

TIPS FOR DOUGHS

Because it mixes and kneads stiff doughs easily, the food processor takes much of the effort out of making yeast breads and fresh pasta. If your processor comes with a special plastic blade designed just for kneading yeast dough, use it when you make bread; otherwise, use the metal blade.

Mixing the dough. What's the right consistency for yeast or pasta dough before kneading? That's a common question among novice cooks. Properly mixed dough should feel just slightly moist. It should look smooth, not dry and crumbly nor wet and overly sticky (see photo 2, page 78). The processor may provide you with a clue, too: if the machine begins to slow down, it could mean that the dough is too sticky and needs another tablespoon or two of flour.

Kneading. Once the dough has been mixed to the right consistency, let the processor knead it. Process for 45 to 60 seconds, but no more—the dough may overheat and work up under the blade. Overprocessing also puts a strain on the machine's motor.

Gougère

1 Stir mixture of milk, butter, and flour vigorously until it leaves sides of pan and forms a heavy ball.

2 Transfer dough to work bowl; with motor running, pour eggs slowly through feed tube. (Without a processor, this step would require vigorous beating by hand.)

3 Continue processing until dough is smooth and well blended. Then add half of the shredded cheese and process until combined.

4 Use an ice cream scoop to mound about ¾ of the dough into a ring on a baking sheet. Then make a small mound atop each big one; sprinkle with cheese.

Gougère

(Pictured on facing page)

When you add Swiss cheese to cream puff dough, you get a golden, puffy, crusty bread called *gougère*. For the best flavor, always serve the savory puffs hot from the oven.

- **4 ounces Swiss cheese**
- **1 cup milk**
- **¼ cup butter or margarine**
- **½ teaspoon salt**
- **Dash of white pepper**
- **1 cup all-purpose flour**
- **4 eggs**

Insert shredding disc. Shred cheese as directed on page 8; set aside.

Change to metal blade. Place milk, butter, salt, and pepper in a 2 to 3-quart pan; bring to a boil over high heat. Add flour all at once; then reduce heat to medium and cook, stirring constantly, until mixture leaves sides of pan and forms a ball (about 2 minutes).

Spoon dough into work bowl. Place eggs in a measuring cup. With motor running, slowly pour eggs through feed tube and continue processing until dough is smooth and well blended (about 30 seconds after last egg is added). Add ½ cup of the cheese to work bowl; process continuously until combined.

With a large spoon, scoop out three-fourths of the dough in 6 to 8 equal portions; arrange in a circle on a greased baking sheet, sides barely touching. Scoop out remaining dough in 6 to 8 smaller mounds; then place one atop each of the larger mounds. Evenly sprinkle with remaining cheese.

Bake on center rack in a 375° oven until puffs are lightly browned and crisp (50 to 55 minutes). Serve hot. Makes 4 to 6 servings.

Petites Brioches

A French breakfast table wouldn't be complete without rich and buttery brioches, sweet butter, and steaming cups of *café au lait*. But brioches complement other meals equally well—consider serving them at lunch or supper, with soup and salad or an omelet.

- **½ cup (¼ lb.) butter, cut into chunks**
- **1 package active dry yeast**
- **½ cup warm water (about 110°)**
- **2 teaspoons sugar**
- **1 teaspoon salt**
- **3 eggs**
- **About 3½ cups all-purpose flour**
- **1 egg yolk beaten with 1 tablespoon milk**

Let butter stand at room temperature until soft.

Insert metal blade or plastic dough blade. Place yeast, water, and sugar in work bowl; process just to combine. Let stand until bubbly (about 10 minutes). Add salt and eggs to work bowl and process just to combine. Add butter and 3½ cups of the flour; process continuously until dough forms a ball, then stop machine. Dough should be slightly moist. (If it's too wet, add more flour, 1 tablespoon at a time, processing after each addition.) Process continuously for about 45 seconds to knead (dough should be smooth and satiny).

Place dough in a greased bowl; turn to grease top. Cover; let rise in a warm place until doubled (1 to 2 hours). Punch dough down; knead briefly on a floured board. Return to greased bowl; turn to grease top. Cover with plastic wrap; refrigerate for at least 12 or up to 24 hours.

Turn dough out onto a lightly floured board and knead briefly. Divide into 12 equal portions if using 3 to 4-inch petite brioche tins or 3-inch muffin cups; divide into 16 equal portions if using 2½-inch muffin cups. Dough is easiest to handle if kept cold, so shape a few brioches at a time, keeping remaining dough refrigerated.

Use one portion of dough for each brioche. Pinch off about a sixth of dough portion and set aside; shape remainder into a smooth ball by pulling surface of dough to underside of ball. Pinch ball at bottom to seal, then place, smooth side up, in a well-greased petite brioche tin or muffin cup. Press dough down to cover pan bottom evenly. Shape reserved small piece of dough into a smooth teardrop. With your finger, poke a hole in center of brioche dough in pan and insert pointed end of teardrop; settle it in securely, or it may pop off during baking.

Cover pans and let stand in a warm place until dough has almost doubled (1 to 2 hours). Brush tops of brioches with egg yolk mixture. (Don't let mixture accumulate at base of topknot; this would prevent proper rising.)

Bake in a 425° oven until richly browned (15 to 18 minutes.) Remove from pans; serve warm or at room temperature. Makes sixteen 2½-inch brioches or twelve 3 to 4-inch brioches.

Apricot Nut Muffins

The key to making tender, cakelike muffins is to treat the batter with care. As with hand-mixed muffins, overbeating is the pitfall to avoid: be sure to *stop the machine the instant the liquid is incorporated.* Don't worry if the batter looks lumpy. It's lumpy batter that yields perfect muffins.

    1 cup all-purpose flour
    ½ cup sugar
    1 tablespoon baking powder
    ½ teaspoon salt
    ¼ cup butter or margarine, cut into chunks
    ⅓ cup *each* dried apricots and walnut halves
    1 egg
    1 cup milk

Insert metal blade. Place flour, sugar, baking powder, salt, and butter in work bowl. Process continuously until mixture resembles fine crumbs. Add apricots and walnuts to work bowl. In a measuring cup, beat egg lightly with milk. With motor running, pour mixture through feed tube; continue processing just until liquid is incorporated (batter will be lumpy). *Do not overprocess.* Spoon into 12 greased or paper-lined 2½-inch muffin cups. Bake in a 375° oven until tops are browned and spring back when lightly touched (20 to 25 minutes). Makes 1 dozen muffins.

Orange Date Scones

British cousins to our biscuits, scones are made in numerous versions. These are flavored with dates and orange peel, and sprinkled with sugar before baking for a sweet, crunchy top crust.

    2 cups all-purpose flour
    1 tablespoon baking powder
    2 tablespoons plus 2 teaspoons sugar
    ½ teaspoon *each* salt and grated orange peel
    ¼ cup butter or margarine, cut into chunks
    ¼ cup firmly packed pitted dates
    2 eggs
    ⅓ cup whipping cream

Insert metal blade. Place flour, baking powder, 2 tablespoons of the sugar, salt, and orange peel in work bowl; process just to combine. Add butter

and process continuously until mixture resembles fine crumbs. Place dates in work bowl.

Reserve 1 tablespoon egg white; then lightly beat remaining eggs and cream in a measuring cup. With motor running, pour mixture through feed tube and continue processing just until dough begins to hold together.

Turn dough out onto a lightly floured board; gather into a ball with your hands, then divide in half. Gently pat each half into a circle about ½ inch thick and 6 inches in diameter. Cut each circle into 4 wedges; place wedges about 1 inch apart on an ungreased baking sheet. Brush tops of scones with reserved egg white and sprinkle with remaining 2 teaspoons sugar.

Bake in a 400° oven until golden brown (about 15 minutes). Serve warm. Makes 8 scones.

Herbed Stuffing Bread

As the name implies, this bread is wonderful for poultry stuffing; it makes savory sandwiches, too. The aroma will make you think of a plump Thanksgiving turkey.

    1 package active dry yeast
    1 teaspoon sugar
    ¾ cup warm water (about 110°)
    2 tablespoons salad oil
      About 2¾ cups all-purpose flour
    ½ cup yellow cornmeal
    1 teaspoon salt
    2 tablespoons toasted instant minced onion
    1 teaspoon celery seeds
    ¾ teaspoon *each* rubbed sage and dry rosemary
    ¼ teaspoon pepper
    1 egg

In a measuring cup, dissolve yeast and sugar in water; let stand until bubbly (about 10 minutes). Stir in oil.

Insert metal blade or plastic dough blade. Place 2½ cups of the flour, cornmeal, salt, onion, celery seeds, sage, rosemary, and pepper in work bowl; process just to combine. Add egg to work bowl. Then, with motor running, pour yeast mixture through feed tube in a steady stream, as fast as flour absorbs it. When dough forms a ball, stop machine. Dough should be slightly moist. (If it's too wet, add up to ¼ cup more flour, 1 tablespoon at a time, processing after each addition.) Process continuously for 45 seconds to knead.

Shape dough into a ball, place in a greased bowl, and turn to grease top. Cover and let rise in a warm place until doubled (1½ to 2 hours).

Punch down dough, knead briefly on a floured board, and shape into a smooth loaf. Place in a greased 4½ by 8½-inch loaf pan. Cover and let rise in a warm place until dough has risen 1¼ inches above pan rim (about 45 minutes).

Bake in a 375° oven until browned (about 35 minutes). Turn out onto a rack to cool. Makes 1 loaf.

Whole Wheat Country Loaf

This nutty whole wheat loaf owes its rustic, country-style look to slashes made in the risen dough before baking. In addition to adding a decorative touch, the cuts allow steam to escape while the bread bakes, so it won't crack.

1 **package active dry yeast**
1 **teaspoon sugar**
1 **cup warm water (about 110°)**
1 **tablespoon salad oil**
2 **tablespoons molasses**
1¾ **cups whole wheat flour**
  About 1¼ cups all-purpose flour
¼ **cup wheat germ**
1 **teaspoon salt**
1 **egg white beaten with 2 teaspoons water**

In a measuring cup, dissolve yeast and sugar in water; let stand until bubbly (about 10 minutes). Stir in oil and molasses; set mixture aside.

Insert metal blade or plastic dough blade. Place whole wheat flour, 1 cup of the all-purpose flour, wheat germ, and salt in work bowl; process just to combine. With motor running, pour yeast mixture through feed tube in a steady stream, as fast as flour absorbs it. When dough forms a ball, stop machine. Dough should be slightly moist. (If it's too wet, add up to ¼ cup more all-purpose flour, 1 tablespoon at a time, processing after each addition.) Process continuously for 45 seconds to knead.

Shape dough into a ball, place in a greased bowl, and turn to grease top. Cover; let rise in a warm place until doubled (about 1½ hours).

Punch down dough, knead briefly on a floured board, and shape into a smooth, 10-inch-long oblong. Place on a greased baking sheet. Cover; let rise until almost doubled (about 45 minutes).

With a razor blade or a sharp knife, cut 3 lengthwise slashes, ½ inch deep, in center and along outside edges of loaf. Brush loaf lightly with egg white mixture. Bake in a 375° oven until browned (about 35 minutes). Let cool on a rack. Makes 1 loaf.

Cornmeal Cheddar Bread

A handful of sharp Cheddar, a touch of hot pepper, and a sprinkling of cornmeal combine to produce a homey, country-style loaf. Toasting brings out the bread's cheese flavor, making it a natural companion for eggs.

1 **package active dry yeast**
2 **tablespoons sugar**
1 **cup warm water (about 110°)**
4 **ounces sharp Cheddar cheese, cut into chunks**
  About 3½ cups all-purpose flour
½ **cup yellow cornmeal**
1 **teaspoon salt**
½ **to 1 teaspoon crushed red pepper**
1 **egg**

In a measuring cup, dissolve yeast and 1 teaspoon of the sugar in water; let stand until bubbly (about 10 minutes).

Insert metal blade. Place cheese in work bowl; process, using on-off pulses, until coarsely chopped. Leave in work bowl. Add remaining sugar, 3¼ cups of the flour, cornmeal, salt, and pepper; process just to combine. Add egg to work bowl; then, with motor running, pour yeast mixture through feed tube in a steady stream, as fast as flour absorbs it. When dough forms a ball, stop machine. Dough should be slightly moist. (If it's too wet, add up to ¼ cup more flour, 1 tablespoon at a time, processing after each addition.) Process continuously for 45 seconds to knead (dough should be smooth and satiny).

Shape dough into a ball, place in a greased bowl, and turn to grease top. Cover and let rise in a warm place until doubled (1 to 1½ hours).

Punch down dough and knead briefly on a lightly floured board. Shape into a smooth ball; then place on a greased baking sheet and flatten to make a 7-inch round. Cover and let rise in a warm place until loaf is about 2½ inches high (about 1 hour). Sprinkle top lightly with flour.

Bake in 375° oven until well browned (about 35 minutes). Let cool on a rack. Makes 1 loaf.

Crusty French Bread

The simplest of ingredients—flour, water, and yeast—combine to create a golden loaf with an elastic texture. The crisp, chewy crust results from a two-part treatment: the loaf is first brushed with a cornstarch glaze to give it chewiness and gloss, then baked in a steamy oven for extra crustiness.

  1 **package active dry yeast**
  1 **teaspoon sugar**
  1 **cup warm water (about 110°)**
  About 3¼ cups all-purpose flour or bread flour
  1 **teaspoon salt**
  Cornmeal
  1 **teaspoon cornstarch**
  ½ **cup water**

In a measuring cup, dissolve yeast and sugar in the 1 cup warm water; let stand until bubbly (about 10 minutes).

Insert metal blade or plastic dough blade. Place 3¼ cups of the flour and salt in work bowl and process just to combine. With motor running, pour yeast mixture through feed tube in a steady stream, as fast as flour absorbs it. When dough forms a ball, stop machine. Dough should be slightly moist. (If it's too wet, add more flour, 1 tablespoon at a time, processing after each addition.) Process continuously for 45 seconds to knead.

Shape dough into a ball, place in a greased bowl, and turn to grease top. Cover and let rise in a warm place until doubled (1 to 1½ hours).

Punch down dough and knead briefly on a lightly floured board; then divide in half. Shape each half by rolling it back and forth, elongating it into a 15-inch-long loaf. Tuck ends of each loaf under; pinch to seal. Place loaves, side by side, on a greased and cornmeal-dusted baking sheet. Cover; let rise until doubled (about 1 hour).

Adjust oven racks to the 2 lowest positions. Preheat oven to 425°. Just before bread is ready to bake, place a 10 by 15-inch rimmed baking pan on lower rack and pour in boiling water to a depth of about ¼ inch. Meanwhile, place cornstarch and the ½ cup water in a small pan; bring to a boil over high heat, then stir well and let cool slightly. With a razor blade or a sharp knife, cut ½-inch-deep diagonal slashes at 1½ to 2-inch intervals on top of risen loaves; then brush with some of the cornstarch mixture.

Bake for 10 minutes. Brush again with cornstarch mixture and continue baking until loaves are golden and sound hollow when tapped (about 15 more minutes). Let cool on racks. Makes 2 loaves.

Dark & Hearty Rye Bread

(Pictured on facing page)

Serve thin slices of this close-textured bread with a selection of cold meats and cheeses for make-your-own sandwiches. Or just spread slices with sweet butter and enjoy as a snack.

  1 **package active dry yeast**
  1 **teaspoon sugar**
  1 **cup warm water (about 110°)**
  2 **tablespoons salad oil**
  3 **tablespoons dark molasses**
  ½ **ounce unsweetened chocolate**
  1 **tablespoon caraway seeds**
  ½ **teaspoon fennel seeds**
  ¾ **cup shredded bran cereal**
  1 **teaspoon salt**
  1½ **cups rye flour**
  About 1¾ cups all-purpose flour

In a measuring cup, dissolve yeast and sugar in water; let stand until bubbly (about 10 minutes). Stir in oil and molasses; set aside.

Insert metal blade. Place chocolate, caraway seeds, fennel seeds, bran cereal, and salt in work bowl. Process continuously until chocolate is finely chopped; leave in work bowl. Add rye flour and 1¾ cups of the all-purpose flour to work bowl. With motor running, pour yeast mixture through feed tube in a steady stream, as fast as flour absorbs it. When dough forms a ball, stop machine. Dough should be slightly moist. (If it's too wet, add more all-purpose flour, 1 tablespoon at a time, processing after each addition.) Process continuously for 45 seconds to knead.

Shape dough into a ball; place in a greased bowl and turn to grease top. Cover and let rise in a warm place until doubled (1 to 1½ hours).

Punch down dough and knead briefly on a lightly floured board, then shape into a smooth ball. Place on a greased baking sheet. Flatten slightly to make a 6-inch round. Cover and let rise until loaf is 2½ inches high (about 45 minutes). Bake in a 375° oven until well browned (about 35 minutes). Let cool on a rack. Makes 1 loaf.

Dark & Hearty Rye Bread

1 Pour dissolved yeast, oil, and molasses through feed tube while dry ingredients whirl in work bowl.

2 When dough forms a ball, stop machine. Pinch dough with your fingers to determine texture—dough should be moist and pliant, but not overly sticky (see photo 2, page 78).

3 To see if dough has risen long enough, poke it with 2 fingers. If indentations remain, dough is ready to be shaped.

4 Measure dough to check second rising. If loaf is about twice as tall as when it was shaped, it's ready to be baked.

Desserts

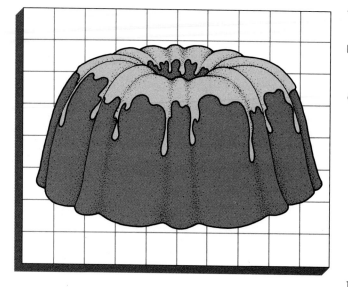

Pineapple-Coconut Bars

⌀ Tropical fruits add sweet succulence and chewy texture to these bar cookies.

- ¾ cup all-purpose flour
- ¾ teaspoon baking powder
- ½ teaspoon salt
- ½ cup (¼ lb.) butter or margarine, cut into chunks
- 1 cup firmly packed brown sugar
- 2 eggs
- ¼ teaspoon almond extract
- ¾ cup sweetened flaked coconut
- 1 can (8 oz.) crushed pineapple packed in its own juice, drained well

Insert metal blade. Place flour, baking powder, and salt in work bowl; process just to combine. Set aside.

With motor running, drop butter through feed tube, one chunk at a time. Add brown sugar to work bowl and process continuously (stopping to scrape bowl once or twice) until mixture is soft and smooth. Place eggs and almond extract in a measuring cup; with motor running, pour through feed tube and continue processing until light and fluffy. Add flour mixture to work bowl and process, using on-off pulses, just until combined. Add coconut and pineapple and process, using on-off pulses, just until combined.

Pour into a lightly greased and flour-dusted 9-inch square baking pan. Bake in a 350° oven until top springs back when lightly pressed (25 to 30 minutes). Transfer to a rack; loosen edges with a spatula, then let cool completely. Cut into 1 by 2¼-inch bars. Makes 3 dozen bars.

Fresh Apricot Soup

This unusual soup is cool, refreshing, and easy to prepare. Serve it for a sophisticated dessert or brunch dish.

1½ **pounds apricots, quartered and pitted**
1 **cup** *each* **water and dry white wine**
1 **cinnamon stick (about 2 inches long)**
1½ **tablespoons lemon juice**
¾ **to 1 cup granulated sugar**
1 **tablespoon** *each* **cornstarch and water, stirred together**
¼ **cup apricot or almond liqueur (optional)**
1 **cup whipping cream, sour cream, or plain yogurt**
Powdered sugar

Place apricots in a 4-quart pan with water, wine, cinnamon stick, and lemon juice. Bring to a boil over high heat; then cover, reduce heat, and simmer until fruit mashes easily (about 15 minutes).

Remove from heat and discard cinnamon stick. Insert metal blade. With a slotted spoon, transfer fruit (leaving liquid in pan) to work bowl; process continuously until puréed. (At this point, you may let purée cool completely, cover and refrigerate until cold, and then freeze for up to 4 months. Thaw before continuing.)

Return purée to pan; stir in granulated sugar and cornstarch mixture. Cook over high heat, stirring, until mixture thickens (about 5 minutes). Remove from heat and let cool slightly. Skim off and discard any foam. Add liqueur (if used) and half the cream; whisk into soup to incorporate smoothly. (If using sour cream or yogurt, stir until smooth before adding.) Let soup cool; cover and refrigerate for at least 6 hours.

Just before serving, insert metal blade. Thicken remaining cream as directed on page 8 (or whip cream by hand). Sweeten cream (or remaining sour cream or yogurt) to taste with powdered sugar; spoon into a bowl. Pass sweetened cream and powdered sugar to add to each portion. Makes about 4½ cups.

Cherry Soup

Follow directions for **Apricot Soup,** but substitute 1½ pounds **Bing cherries** (pitted) for apricots and use **kirsch** in place of liqueur (if desired). Reduce granulated sugar to ¼ to ⅓ cup. Makes about 4 cups.

Profiteroles

Airy cream puffs are filled with a scoop of ice cream and topped with either dark chocolate or fresh strawberry sauce. For entertaining ease, the puffs can be baked, split, and filled with ice cream hours before serving.

12 **medium-size or 24 small Cream puffs (recipe follows)**
Vanilla, coffee, mint, or nut ice cream
Bittersweet chocolate sauce or Strawberry sauce (page 95)

Prepare cream puffs. Let cool, then cut in half crosswise. Fill each puff with your choice of ice cream. If made ahead, cover and freeze for up to 8 hours; let stand at room temperature for 10 minutes before serving.

Prepare sauce of your choice. For each serving, place 1 medium-size or 2 or 3 small puffs in a small, shallow-rimmed bowl; top with about 2 tablespoons of sauce. Makes 8 to 12 servings.

Cream puffs. Place 1 cup **water,** ½ cup (¼ lb.) **butter** or margarine, ¼ teaspoon **salt,** and 1 teaspoon **sugar** in a 3-quart pan. Bring to a boil over high heat, stirring constantly to melt butter. Add 1 cup **all-purpose flour** all at once; reduce heat to medium and stir rapidly until dough leaves sides of pan and forms a ball (1 to 2 minutes).

Insert metal blade. Spoon dough into work bowl. Place 4 **eggs** in a measuring cup. With motor running, slowly pour eggs through feed tube and continue processing until well mixed (about 30 seconds after last egg is added).

To shape cream puffs, use a pastry bag fitted with a plain tip or a spoon. Use about 2 tablespoons dough for each medium-size puff and about 1 tablespoon for each small puff. Place mounds 2 inches apart on greased baking sheets. Beat 1 **egg** with 1 teaspoon **water.** Brush egg mixture lightly over tops of puffs, being sure glaze does not drip down sides of puffs onto baking sheet (this prevents proper rising).

Bake in upper third of a 425° oven for 15 minutes. Reduce heat to 375°. Cut a slash in bottom of each puff, then continue baking until puffs are firm, dry to the touch, and golden brown (about 10 more minutes). Let cool on racks. Wrap airtight and store at room temperature for up to 24 hours; or freeze for up to 1 month. Makes about 2 dozen medium-size or 3 to 4 dozen small puffs.

(Continued on page 95)

Strawberry Ice

1 Sweeten purée of fresh ripe strawberries with sugar, then add lemon juice for tang.

2 Pour purée into ice cube trays to freeze (it's easier and neater to pour from a large measuring cup than from work bowl).

3 Puréeing frozen cubes breaks up ice cystals, gives you a soft, smooth mixture with a consistency reminiscent of fruit slush.

4 Spoon frozen purée into a baking pan or plastic freezer container. Return to freezer until solid; purée again just before serving.

Bittersweet chocolate sauce. Insert metal blade. Place 4 ounces **unsweetened chocolate,** cut into chunks, in work bowl. Process until finely chopped; use on-off pulses at first, then process continuously. Place ½ cup **water,** ¾ to 1 cup **sugar,** and 1 teaspoon **vanilla** in a small pan; bring to a boil over high heat. With motor running, pour liquid through feed tube and continue processing until smooth. Makes about 1½ cups.

Strawberry sauce. Insert metal blade. Place 2 cups hulled **strawberries,** ¼ cup **sugar,** and 2 tablespoons **lemon juice** in work bowl. Process continuously until smooth. Makes about 1½ cups.

Strawberry Ice

(Pictured on facing page)

Long popular in Europe, intensely flavored fruit ices offer a light, refreshing close to hot-weather meals.

- **4 cups hulled strawberries**
- **½ cup *each* sugar and water**
- **2 tablespoons lemon juice**
  Garnishes: Fan wafers, or lemon, lime, or orange slices or zest

Insert metal blade. Process strawberries continuously until puréed. Add sugar, water, and lemon juice; process just to combine. Pour purée into ice cube trays and freeze until solid; transfer to plastic bags and freeze for up to 2 weeks.

Process about 6 cubes of purée at a time (or more in a large-capacity processor). Use on-off pulses at first to break up cubes, then process continuously until mixture is soft and smooth. Transfer to a 9-inch square pan, cover, and freeze until solid (at least 4 hours) or for up to 1 week.

To serve, insert metal blade. Place ice in work bowl (a portion at a time, if necessary) and process until smooth and free of ice crystals. Serve immediately, garnished as desired. Makes 3 cups.

Blackberry Ice

Insert metal blade. Process 2 cups fresh or frozen unsweetened **blackberries** until puréed. Pour into a wire strainer; stir with a spoon to force juice through. Discard seeds. Return purée to work bowl; add ½ cup **sugar,** 2 tablespoons **lemon** juice, and ½ cup **water.** Process for 2 seconds to mix. Freeze and serve as directed for **Strawberry Ice.** Makes about 2 cups.

Lemon Ice

Cut zest (colored outer layer of peel) from 1 small **lemon;** cut zest into ½-inch pieces. Insert metal blade. Place zest and 1 cup **sugar** in work bowl; process continuously until zest is finely chopped. Place mixture in a 3-quart pan; add 3 cups **water** and a dash of **salt.** Heat, stirring, just until sugar is dissolved. Let cool, then stir in ⅔ cup **lemon juice.** Freeze and serve as directed for **Strawberry Ice.** Makes about 3½ cups.

Pineapple Ice

(Pictured on facing page)

Peel and core 1 large **pineapple;** cut into chunks. Insert metal blade. Place pineapple chunks in work bowl, half at a time (or all at once in a large-capacity processor); process continuously until puréed. You should have a total of 4 cups purée. Stir in 1 cup **water,** 2 tablespoons **sugar** (or to taste), and 2 tablespoons **lemon juice.** Freeze and serve as directed for **Strawberry Ice.** Makes about 5 cups.

Papaya Ice

(Pictured on facing page)

Peel, halve, and seed 1 large **papaya.** Cut each half into quarters. Insert metal blade. Process papaya continuously until puréed; you should have 1¼ cups. Add 2 tablespoons **lime juice,** 3 tablespoons **sugar,** and ⅓ cup **water.** Freeze and serve as directed for **Strawberry Ice.** Makes 1⅔ cups.

Caffè Granita

In a mixing bowl, stir together 2 cups cold, strong **coffee** and ½ cup **coffee, orange, or almond liqueur.** Freeze and purée as directed for **Strawberry Ice.** To serve, pour equal portions of coffee ice into four 8-ounce glasses. To each glass, add 1 or 2 scoops **vanilla ice cream.** Top each serving with about ¼ cup **sweetened thickened cream** (page 8) or whipped cream and 1 **chocolate-covered coffee bean.** Makes 4 servings.

If you enjoy confections based on nut pastes, you might consider making your own from almonds or hazelnuts. The food processor easily makes nut butters, too.

Most of the nuts sold in supermarkets have already been roasted; for best results, use oil-roasted rather then dry-roasted nuts. Even if you start with roasted nuts, an extra toasting will give you the richest-tasting butters.

Toasted Nut Paste

1 pound (about 3 cups) whole or large pieces of hazelnuts (filberts) or blanched almonds
2 cups powdered sugar
5 to 6 tablespoons lightly beaten egg whites

Spread nuts on a 10 by 15-inch rimmed baking sheet and toast in a 350° oven until pale gold (10 to 15 minutes). If using hazelnuts, pour hot nuts onto a dishtowel and fold to enclose. Rub briskly to remove as much of skins as possible, then lift nuts from cloth. Let nuts cool.

Insert metal blade. Place cooled nuts in work bowl and coarsely chop as directed on page 12. Then remove about two-thirds of the chopped nuts from bowl. Process nuts remaining in bowl until mealy; set aside. Return remaining chopped nuts to bowl, half at a time, and process until mealy.

Return all nuts to work bowl. Add powdered sugar. With motor running, add 5 tablespoons of the egg whites. Process continuously just until mixture begins to hold together. Add more egg whites if needed. Wrap in plastic wrap and refrigerate for at least 1 hour or for up to 2 weeks. Makes 2 to 3 cups.

Chocolate-dipped Bonbons. Prepare **Toasted Nut Paste** (this page); you'll need about 2 cups. Shape 1-tablespoon portions of nut paste into 1-inch balls; flatten bottoms slightly and set 1 inch apart on 10 by 15-inch rimmed baking sheets lined with wax paper.

Place 6 ounces **semisweet chocolate chips** in the top of a double boiler over simmering water; stir just until melted. Dip each ball into chocolate to coat top half. Return to paper-lined pans, chocolate side up. Refrigerate, uncovered, until chocolate is set (about 30 minutes). Serve, or cover and refrigerate for up to 1 week. Let stand at room temperature for about 15 minutes before serving. Makes about 3 dozen.

Nut Butter

About 1½ cups unsalted peanuts, blanched almonds, cashews, or pecans
Salt (optional)

Place nuts in work bowl. Use on-off pulses at first to chop nuts (scraping bowl once or twice); then process continuously until very smooth and creamy. (If you prefer a crunchy nut butter, stop processing when mixture reaches desired consistency.) Add salt to taste, if desired. Makes about 1 cup.

Toasted nut butter. Spread 1½ cups **peanuts, blanched almonds, cashews, hazelnuts (filberts), or pecans** on a rimmed baking sheet. Toast in a 350° oven for 5 to 10 minutes for peanuts or cashews, 10 to 15 minutes for almonds or hazelnuts, or 8 to 10 minutes for pecans. (If peanuts or cashews are raw, toast peanuts for 10 to 15 minutes, cashews for 15 to 20 minutes.) If using hazelnuts, remove skins as directed for **Toasted Nut Paste** (this page).

Let nuts cool to room temperature, then process as directed for **Nut Butter.**

Fresh Fruit-topped Pastry

𝄐 With the aid of a food processor, you can quickly and easily create professional-looking pastries. Both crust and filling can be prepared in minutes; the topping is simply sliced fresh fruit, finished with a glaze of melted jelly.

> **Sour cream pastry (recipe follows)**
> **Cheese or almond filling (recipes follow)**
> ⅓ **cup red currant jelly or orange marmalade**
> **About 4½ cups hulled, halved strawberries or sliced apricots, peaches, or kiwi (or use 2¼ cups *each* of 2 different fruits)**

Prepare pastry. While pastry chills, prepare filling of your choice and set aside.

On a floured board, roll pastry out to an 8 by 11-inch rectangle, about ⅜ inch thick. Place on an ungreased baking sheet. Spoon filling down center of pastry; spread to within 1½ inches of long sides. Fold long sides over to cover edges of filling.

Bake in a 425° oven until browned (12 to 15 minutes). Let cool completely. (At this point, you may cover loosely with foil and let stand at room temperature for up to 4 hours.)

Up to 1 hour before serving, melt jelly in a small pan over low heat (use jelly with strawberries or kiwi, marmalade with apricots or peaches). Lightly brush filling with some of the melted jelly. Arrange fruit over filling, overlapping pieces slightly. Brush fruit with remaining jelly. Cut with a sharp knife. Makes 8 to 10 servings.

Sour cream pastry. Insert metal blade. Place 1 cup **all-purpose flour** and ½ cup (¼ lb.) **butter** or margarine (cut into chunks) in work bowl. Process continuously until mixture resembles fine crumbs. Stir together 3 tablespoons **sour cream** and 1 **egg yolk.** Add to work bowl and process, using on-off pulses, just until mixture begins to hold together (don't let it form a ball). Wrap dough in plastic wrap and refrigerate until firm (at least 1 hour) or for up to 3 days; or freeze for up to 1 month (thaw before using).

Cheese filling. Cut four ½ by 1-inch strips of **lemon zest** (colored outer layer of peel). Cut 8 ounces **cream cheese** into chunks.

Insert metal blade. With motor running, drop zest and cream cheese through feed tube; continue processing until zest is finely chopped. Add ⅓ cup **sugar,** 2 tablespoons **all-purpose flour,** and 1 teaspoon **vanilla** to work bowl. Process continuously (stopping to scrape bowl once or twice) until smooth.

Almond filling. Cut ¼ cup **butter** or margarine into chunks; cut four ½ by 1-inch strips of **lemon zest** (colored outer layer of peel).

Insert metal blade. With motor running, drop zest and butter (one chunk at a time) through feed tube; continue processing until zest is finely chopped. Add 1 package (7 oz.) **almond paste** (or ¾ cup homemade almond paste, page 96) and 1 **egg white** to work bowl; process continuously until blended.

Apple Crisp

𝄐 ⊖ Slice apples in seconds, make a buttery topping with the flick of a switch . . . then put it all together. The result? A homey and old-fashioned dessert favorite. For a change of pace, use pears instead of apples.

> ½ **cup walnut halves**
> 1 **cup sugar**
> 1 **teaspoon ground cinnamon**
> ½ **teaspoon ground nutmeg**
> ½ **cup raisins**
> ¾ **cup all-purpose flour**
> ⅓ **cup butter or margarine, cut into chunks**
> 8 **small, firm red apples (2½ to 3 lbs. *total*)**
> 1 **tablespoon lemon juice**
> **Half-and-half (light cream)**

Insert metal blade. Place walnuts, ½ cup of the sugar, cinnamon, and nutmeg in work bowl. Process continuously until walnuts are coarsely chopped; transfer mixture to a large bowl and stir in raisins.

Place flour, remaining ½ cup sugar, and butter in work bowl. Process, using on-off pulses, until mixture is evenly crumbly; set aside.

Change to slicing disc. Peel and core apples, then slice as directed on page 8. Add apples and lemon juice to walnut mixture; stir until well combined. Turn into a 9-inch square baking pan. Sprinkle flour mixture evenly over apples. Bake, uncovered, in a 400° oven until apples are tender when pierced and top is browned (about 45 minutes). Serve warm or at room temperature. Pass half-and-half to pour over individual servings. Makes 6 to 8 servings.

Fresh Raspberry Tartlets

(Pictured on facing page)

𝄐 Sweet-tart lemon curd, spread on plain cookies, is a favorite English teatime treat. We've developed a delicate raspberry version as a special filling for tartlet shells; you could also spoon it over fresh fruit or spread it on toasted English muffins or ginger wafers.

- 1 **cup fresh or frozen unsweetened raspberries**
- 2 **tablespoons lemon juice**
- ½ **cup (¼ lb.) butter or margarine**
- 3 **tablespoons sugar**
- 4 **eggs**
  - **Red food color (optional)**
  - **Press-in pastry (recipe follows)**
  - **Fresh raspberries and fresh mint sprigs**

Insert metal blade. Place the 1 cup raspberries and lemon juice in work bowl and process continuously until puréed. Pour into a wire strainer set over a measuring cup; stir with a spoon to force juice through. Discard seeds (you should have ½ cup purée).

Melt butter in a 2 to 3-quart pan over medium heat; add raspberry purée, sugar, and eggs. Reduce heat to low. Using a wire whisk, stir constantly until mixture is smooth and thickened (about 10 minutes). For a deeper color, stir in food color, a few drops at a time, until mixture is the shade desired. Let cool; cover and refrigerate until thickened (at least 1 hour or for up to 1 week).

Meanwhile, prepare press-in pastry. For each tartlet, place a rounded tablespoon of pastry dough in a medium-size muffin cup (about 2 inches in diameter) or tartlet pan that holds about 3 tablespoons; you'll need 10 to 12 muffin cups or tartlet pans. Press pastry to form an even layer over bottom and up sides of pans; prick lightly with a fork. Bake in a 300° oven until golden (about 25 minutes). Let cool in pans, invert, and carefully tap to release; then turn right side up. If made ahead, cover loosely with foil and store at room temperature until next day.

To serve, place about 2½ tablespoons of the curd in each tartlet shell; top with raspberries. Garnish with mint. Makes 10 to 12 tartlets.

Press-in pastry. Insert metal blade. Place 1 cup **all-purpose flour** and 2 tablespoons **sugar** in work bowl; process just to combine. Cut 6 tablespoons **butter** or margarine into chunks; add to work bowl. Process continuously until mixture resembles coarse meal. Add 1 **egg yolk** to work bowl; process continuously just until mixture begins to hold together. (Don't let it form a ball.) Remove mixture from bowl and work with your hands until it forms a smooth, noncrumbly ball.

Summer Fruit Cobbler

◔𝄐 Summer's stone fruits bake to perfection in this homey cobbler. Serve it after a barbecue, topped with vanilla or nut ice cream.

- 2 **pounds firm-ripe peaches or nectarines (or some of each), halved and pitted**
  - **About ¾ cup sugar**
- 2 **tablespoons lemon juice**
- 1 **teaspoon** *each* **ground nutmeg and vanilla**
- 1 **cup all-purpose flour**
- 1 **teaspoon baking powder**
- ¼ **teaspoon salt**
- ⅓ **cup solid vegetable shortening**
- 3 **tablespoons cold water**
- 2 **tablespoons cornstarch**
- 2 **tablespoons butter or margarine**
  - **Ice cream**

Insert slicing disc. Slice peaches as directed on page 9. Transfer to a large bowl and stir in ¾ cup of the sugar, lemon juice, nutmeg, and vanilla.

Wipe work bowl dry with a paper towel; insert metal blade. Place flour, baking powder, and salt in work bowl; process just to combine. Add shortening and process, using on-off pulses, until mixture resembles fine crumbs. With motor running, pour water through feed tube and process until mixture forms a ball. Dust dough lightly with flour; wrap in plastic wrap.

Spoon liquid from fruit (you should have ½ to ¾ cup); stir in cornstarch until smooth. Stir cornstarch mixture into fruit, then pour mixture into an 8-inch square baking pan. Dot with butter.

On a lightly floured board, roll out dough to a thickness of ⅜ inch. Using a 2½ to 3-inch cookie cutter, cut out shapes and place, close together, on top of fruit mixture. Re-roll excess dough and cut out more shapes, if needed, to cover top of cobbler. Sprinkle evenly with sugar.

Bake in a 400° oven until top is browned and fruit is bubbly (35 to 40 minutes). Let cool slightly on a rack; serve warm or at room temperature with ice cream. Makes about 8 servings.

Fresh Raspberry Tartlets

1 Process flour, sugar, and butter together until mixture resembles coarse meal; then add egg yolk to work bowl.

2 When pastry collects at one side of work bowl and begins to hold together, stop machine. Further processing would toughen pastry.

3 Work mixture into a smooth ball with your hands. With your fingers, press pastry evenly over bottom and up sides of tartlet pans. Prick lightly with a fork before baking.

4 Spoon raspberry curd into baked tartlet shells. Rich, creamy curd and cooky-like pastry shells make a perfect party dessert.

Geometric Shortbread

🍥 We call this flaky shortbread "geometric" because you have a choice of shapes for the finished cookies: squares, rectangles, or triangles.

    1¾ cups all-purpose flour
    ¾ cup cornstarch
        About ½ cup sugar
    1 cup (½ lb.) butter, melted

Insert metal blade. Place flour, cornstarch, and ½ cup of the sugar in work bowl. Process just to combine. With motor running, pour melted butter through feed tube and continue processing (stopping to scrape bowl) until dough holds together.

Press dough evenly into an ungreased 9-inch square baking pan. Bake in a 325° oven until golden (about 50 minutes). While hot, prick surface all over with a fork; sprinkle lightly with additional sugar, then cut with a sharp knife into 24 pieces in one or more shapes. Let cool on a rack, then lift cookies from pan with a spatula. Store airtight for up to 3 days. Makes 2 dozen cookies.

Cookie Pizza

🍥 Our giant cookie pizza is crisp on the outside and chewy in the middle. Instead of anchovies and pepperoni, you top it with nuts and candy.

    ⅓ cup walnut halves
    ½ cup all-purpose flour
    ¼ teaspoon each salt, baking soda, and ground cinnamon
    6 tablespoons butter or margarine, softened
    ½ cup firmly packed brown sugar
    ¼ cup granulated sugar
    1 egg
    ½ teaspoon vanilla
    1 tablespoon milk
    1¼ cups quick-cooking rolled oats
        Toppings (suggestions follow)

Insert metal blade. Chop walnuts as directed on page 12. Add flour, salt, baking soda, and cinnamon; process just to combine. Set aside.

Place butter, brown sugar, and granulated sugar in work bowl; process continuously until combined. With motor running, pour egg, vanilla, and milk through feed tube; continue processing (stopping to scrape bowl once or twice) until mixture is creamy. Add flour mixture; process continuously (stopping to scrape bowl once or twice) just until combined. Add oats; mix into dough, using on-off pulses.

Line a 12-inch pizza pan (or a 14 by 17-inch baking sheet) with foil; grease foil. Spoon batter onto foil and spread to within 1 inch of pan edge (or spread into an 11-inch circle on baking sheet). Sprinkle toppings over batter. Bake in a 350° oven until golden brown (18 to 22 minutes). Let cool in pan on a rack for 10 minutes; then transfer cookie on foil to rack and let cool completely. Cut into wedges to serve. Makes 16 to 20 servings.

Toppings. You'll need a total of ⅓ cup. Choose **chocolate chips,** chopped **nuts,** or **candy-coated plain chocolate candies;** or use some of each.

Powdered Sugar Pound Cake

🍥 Pound cake is delicious plain, but you can easily dress up the buttery slices with ice cream and a spoonful of chocolate or strawberry sauce (page 95).

    1¼ cups all-purpose flour
    ¾ cup (¼ lb. plus ¼ cup) butter or margarine, cut into chunks
    2 cups powdered sugar
    3 eggs
    ½ teaspoon vanilla

Insert metal blade. Place flour in work bowl; process for 5 seconds to sift. Set aside. With motor running, drop butter, one chunk at a time, through feed tube. Continue processing until soft and smooth. Add sugar to work bowl and process continuously (stopping to scrape bowl once or twice) until mixture is light and fluffy.

Place eggs and vanilla in a measuring cup; with motor running, pour slowly through feed tube and continue processing (stopping to scrape bowl once or twice) until creamy. Add flour to work bowl and process, using on-off pulses, just until evenly combined. Pour into a greased 5 by 9-inch loaf pan. Bake in a 325° oven until a wooden pick inserted in center comes out clean (about 1 hour). Let cool in pan for 5 minutes; then turn out onto a rack and let cool completely. Makes 12 to 14 servings.

Carrot Spice Cake

A long-standing favorite, carrot cake is also a natural for food processor preparation. Try our version as a sheet cake spread with cream cheese frosting—or bake it in a tube pan and drizzle with a sweet orange glaze.

- 3 small carrots (about ½ lb. *total*)
- 1 cup walnut or pecan halves
- 3 cups all-purpose flour
- 2½ teaspoons ground cinnamon
- ½ teaspoon *each* ground nutmeg and allspice
- 2 teaspoons baking soda
- 1 tablespoon baking powder
- 5 eggs
- 2 cups sugar
- 1 cup salad oil
- Cream cheese frosting or Orange glaze (recipes follow)

Insert shredding disc. Shred carrots as directed on page 12 (you should have about 2 cups); set aside. Change to metal blade. Finely chop walnuts as directed on page 12; set aside with carrots. Place flour, cinnamon, nutmeg, allspice, baking soda, and baking powder in work bowl; process just to combine. Transfer to a large mixing bowl. Place eggs and sugar in work bowl and process continuously until combined. With motor running, pour oil through feed tube and continue processing until blended. Fold sugar mixture gently into flour mixture. Stir in carrots and walnuts.

Pour batter into a greased 9 by 13-inch baking pan or 10-inch tube pan. Bake in a 350° oven until a wooden pick inserted in center comes out clean (about 40 minutes in a 9 by 13-inch pan; about 1 hour and 15 minutes in a tube pan). Meanwhile, prepare frosting or glaze.

Let sheet cake cool completely, then frost with cream cheese frosting. Or, if using a tube pan, let cool in pan for 15 minutes; turn out onto a rack and let cool completely, then drizzle with glaze. Makes 12 to 16 servings.

Cream cheese frosting. Cut a ½ by 3-inch strip of **orange zest** (colored outer layer of peel); cut strip crosswise into quarters. Cut 6 ounces **cream cheese** and 6 tablespoons **butter** or margarine into chunks. Insert metal blade. With motor running, drop zest, cream cheese, and butter through feed tube and continue processing until

zest is finely chopped. Add 1 teaspoon **vanilla** and 2 cups **powdered sugar** to work bowl; process continuously (stopping to scrape bowl once or twice) until blended.

Orange glaze. Cut a ½ by 3-inch strip of **orange zest** (colored outer layer of peel); cut strip crosswise into quarters. Insert metal blade. Place zest, 2 cups **powdered sugar,** 1 teaspoon **vanilla,** and 3 tablespoons **orange juice** in work bowl; process continuously until zest is finely chopped.

TIPS FOR TENDER PASTRY

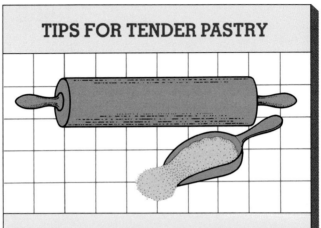

Pie pastry has long been an intimidating prospect to many cooks, troublesome to mix and difficult to shape. But there's really no great mystery to making pastry.

Fat and flour. The food processor cuts butter, margarine, and solid shortening into flour quickly and efficiently. The whirling metal blade swiftly chops the fat into small pieces and distributes them evenly throughout the flour.

When making butter pastry, always use chilled butter (or margarine), cut into even chunks of about 1 tablespoon each.

The final mixing. The addition of liquid, whether egg or water, and the completion of the dough are combined in one quick step. It's important to keep a close eye on the dough in the work bowl, and to *stop the motor as soon as the dough starts to hold together* (see photograph 2 on page 99). Don't let the dough form a ball in the bowl; gather it into a ball with your hands. As in making pastry by hand, restraint in handling is essential; extra processing can overwork and toughen pastry.

Midnight Velvet Torte

1 Pour vinegar-water mixture into frothy egg whites. Vinegar helps stabilize the egg whites; water increases their volume.

2 Process until egg whites hold their shape. Check frequently while processing to ensure that egg whites aren't processed to the point of being overbeaten.

3 To melt chocolate in a food processor, begin by processing chocolate until chopped. Then, with motor running, pour hot liquid through feed tube.

4 Process beaten egg whites and chocolate mixture together just to combine (mixture will appear streaky). Pour into crust-lined pan.

Midnight Velvet Torte

(Pictured on facing page)

Ɓ Dark, rich, and only slightly sweet, this is a chocolate lover's dream come true.

Chocolate crust (recipe follows)
4 eggs, separated
1 tablespoon *each* white (distilled) vinegar and water, stirred together
1 package (12 oz.) semisweet chocolate chips
2 tablespoons sugar
1 teaspoon vanilla
¾ cup milk
2 tablespoons instant coffee
¼ cup coffee liqueur or milk
Chocolate design (directions follow)
Thickened cream (page 8) or whipped cream (optional)

Prepare chocolate crust; set aside. Wash and dry work bowl and metal blade; insert metal blade. Place egg whites in work bowl and process continuously until frothy. With motor running, pour vinegar mixture through feed tube and continue processing until whites hold their shape. Set aside.

Place chocolate chips in work bowl; process until chopped, using on-off pulses. Add egg yolks, sugar, and vanilla. Combine milk and coffee in a small pan over medium heat; stir until scalding. With motor running, pour milk mixture through feed tube; continue processing until chocolate is melted and mixture is smooth. Pour in liqueur and process until combined.

Spoon beaten egg whites into work bowl. Process just until combined, using on-off pulses. Pour mixture into crust-lined pan and refrigerate until firm (at least 4 hours or until next day). Meanwhile, prepare chocolate design.

To serve, remove pan sides. Peel chocolate design off paper; place on top of torte. Cut into small wedges. Garnish with thickened cream, if desired. Makes 10 to 12 servings.

Chocolate crust. Insert metal blade. Crush 20 **chocolate cookie wafers** as directed on page 10. Cut ¼ cup **butter** or margarine into chunks and add to work bowl; process continuously (stopping to scrape bowl once or twice) until combined. Press cookie mixture evenly over bottom of an 8-inch round cake pan with a removable bottom. Bake in a 350° oven for 10 minutes. Let cool on a rack.

Chocolate design. Melt 4 ounces **semisweet chocolate chips** as directed for **Chocolate-dipped Bonbons,** page 96. Draw design on a piece of paper; cover with wax paper. Place chocolate in a pastry bag with a writing tip. Squeeze out chocolate, tracing design. Refrigerate briefly to set.

Amaretto Cheesecake

Ɓ Almonds flavor both the crust and the filling of this creamy cheesecake.

Almond crust (recipe follows)
4 strips lemon zest (colored outer layer of peel), *each* about ½ by 1 inch
1½ pounds cream cheese, cut into chunks
1⅓ cups sugar
4 eggs
2 tablespoons lemon juice
3 tablespoons almond liqueur or 1 teaspoon almond extract
1 teaspoon vanilla
½ cup *each* whipping cream and sour cream

Line bottom of a buttered 5 by 9-inch loaf pan with buttered wax paper. Prepare almond crust; press over bottom and 1 inch up sides of pan.

Insert metal blade. With motor running, drop zest and cream cheese through feed tube; continue processing until zest is coarsely chopped. Add sugar to work bowl and process continuously until combined. Add eggs, lemon juice, liqueur, vanilla, whipping cream, and sour cream to work bowl; process continuously (stopping to scrape bowl) until smooth. Pour into pan. Set pan in a larger pan and pour in 1 inch boiling water.

Bake in a 325° oven until center appears set when pan is gently shaken (about 1 hour and 15 minutes). Lift from water bath and place on a rack; let cool for at least 2 hours. Run a knife around sides of cake. Invert a platter over pan; holding platter in place, invert both. Lift off pan, then peel off paper. Cover cake and refrigerate until cold (at least 5 hours). Makes 12 servings.

Almond crust. Insert metal blade. Process 1½ cups **crisp almond macaroons** continuously until fine crumbs form. Set aside. Finely grind ½ cup **whole blanched almonds** as directed on page 12. Return macaroon crumbs to work bowl. With motor running, drop 3 tablespoons **butter** or margarine (cut into chunks) through feed tube; process until mixture resembles fine crumbs.

Preserves & Relishes

No-cook Strawberry Freezer Jam

This jam couldn't be easier to make—there's no stirring over a hot stove (in fact, there's no cooking at all). The no-cook method gives the jam a brilliant color and an intense fresh strawberry flavor that's wonderful with toast or Petites Brioches (page 87).

- 4 cups strawberries, hulled
- 4 cups sugar
- 2 tablespoons lemon juice
- 1 pouch (3 oz.) liquid pectin

Insert metal blade. Place strawberries in work bowl, half at a time (or all at once in a large-capacity processor); process, using on-off pulses, until coarsely chopped. Transfer to a large mixing bowl. Stir in sugar and let mixture stand for 10 minutes, stirring occasionally.

In a small bowl, stir together lemon juice and pectin; add to berry mixture and stir gently (don't incorporate any air bubbles) for 3 minutes. Ladle into small jars or containers.

Cover and let stand at room temperature until next day, then transfer to the refrigerator. Refrigerate for up to 3 weeks; freeze for longer storage. Makes about 2½ pints.

Short-cook Peach Jam

Ȣ When you make peach jam by the "short-cook" method, you'll get a glossy, medium-soft product with the true, fresh flavor of sweet summer peaches.

- **3 pounds peaches, peeled, quartered, and pitted**
- **¼ cup lemon juice**
- **6 cups sugar**
- **1 pouch (3 oz.) liquid pectin**

Insert metal blade. Place peaches in work bowl, half at a time (or all at once in a large-capacity processor). Process, using on-off pulses, until coarsely chopped. Transfer to an 8 to 10-quart kettle and add lemon juice and sugar. Cook over high heat, stirring constantly, until mixture comes to a rolling boil that can't be stirred down; then boil for exactly 1 minute. Remove from heat and add pectin; stir for 2 to 3 minutes. Skim off foam.

Fill hot sterilized canning jars with jam to within ¼ inch of rims. Wipe rims, then put hot sterilized lids and rings in place. Set jars on a rack in a large kettle and cover with boiling water. Bring water to a simmer; cook for 10 minutes. Makes about 3½ pints.

Three-fruit Marmalade

Ȣ Ƈ Fresh rhubarb is one of the joys of early summer—a joy that's all too fleeting, unless you capture its sweet-tart essence in sprightly preserves like this one. Chopped rhubarb and sliced citrus fruit are cooked together slowly to make a tangy marmalade with a firm texture.

- **2 pounds rhubarb, ends trimmed**
- **3 small lemons**
- **4 large oranges**
- **6 cups sugar**

Insert metal blade. Cut rhubarb into 1-inch chunks. Place in work bowl, about a third at a time; process, using on-off pulses, until coarsely chopped. Transfer to a large mixing bowl.

Change to slicing disc and slice lemons and oranges as directed on page 9. Add to rhubarb, then add sugar; stir to mix well. Cover and refrigerate until next day.

Transfer mixture to a 4 to 5-quart kettle; bring to a boil over high heat, stirring constantly to dissolve sugar. Reduce heat to low and simmer gently, stirring frequently to prevent sticking, until marmalade is thickened (about 1½ hours).

Fill hot sterilized canning jars with marmalade to within ¼ inch of rims. Wipe rims, then put hot sterilized lids and rings in place. Set jars on a rack in a large kettle and cover with boiling water. Bring water to a simmer; cook for 10 minutes. Makes about 4 pints.

Spiced Apple Honey Butter

Ȣ Spiced, honey-sweetened fruit purée, cooked down to concentrate natural fruit sugars, is a delicious spread for muffins, biscuits, or morning toast. There's no need to peel the apples; their skins virtually disappear after long, slow cooking and puréeing.

- **4 pounds tart apples**
- **1 cup water**
- **4 cups apple juice**
- **¼ cup lemon juice**
- **½ teaspoon *each* salt and ground cloves**
- **2 teaspoons ground cinnamon**
- **¼ teaspoon *each* ground ginger and nutmeg**
- **1½ cups light, mild-flavored honey**

Core and quarter unpeeled apples. Place in a 6-quart or larger kettle; add water, apple juice, and lemon juice. Cover and simmer over medium-low heat until apples are soft (about 30 minutes).

Insert metal blade. Transfer apples to work bowl with a slotted spoon, leaving liquid in kettle; process continuously until puréed. (Purée apples a portion at a time in a standard-size processor, all at once in a large-capacity processor.)

Return purée to kettle over low heat. Add salt, cloves, cinnamon, ginger, nutmeg, and honey. Cook, uncovered, for 1 to 1½ hours; stir frequently. As butter thickens, adjust heat and stir often to prevent sticking.

Fill hot sterilized jars with apple butter to within ¼ inch of rims. Wipe rims, then put hot sterilized lids and rings in place. Set jars on a rack in a large kettle and cover with boiling water. Bring water to a simmer; cook for 10 minutes. Makes about 3 pints.

Pear & Ginger Chutney

 Fresh ginger gives this chutney its sweet-hot spiciness. Try serving it alongside cold roasted meats or smoked poultry.

    1 **clove garlic**
      Two 1 by 1-inch chunks fresh ginger
    1 **large onion**
    1 **small lemon**
    5 **to 6 pounds firm-ripe Bartlett pears, peeled, halved, and cored**
 1½ **cups *each* sugar and cider vinegar**
  ½ **teaspoon ground allspice**
  ½ **cup currants**

Insert metal blade. Mince garlic, then ginger as directed on page 13; transfer to a 6-quart kettle. Chop onion as directed on page 13; add to kettle.

Change to slicing disc. Slice lemon as directed on page 9; add to kettle. Slice pears as directed on page 9; add to kettle with sugar, vinegar, allspice, and currants. Bring to a boil over high heat; then reduce heat and simmer, uncovered, stirring often, until almost all juices have evaporated (about 1½ hours).

Fill hot sterilized jars to within ¼ inch of rims. Wipe rims; then put hot sterilized lids and rings in place. Set jars on a rack in a large kettle and cover with boiling water. Bring water to a simmer; cook for 10 minutes. Makes about 3½ pints.

Cranberry Orange Relish

 This tangy relish is a tasty partner for roast poultry or pork.

    1 **large orange (unpeeled), cut into chunks**
   12 **ounces cranberries**
    1 **cup sugar**
    1 **tablespoon lemon juice**

Insert metal blade. Place orange in work bowl. Process, using on-off pulses, until finely chopped; transfer to a 3-quart pan. Place cranberries in work bowl and process, using on-off pulses, until finely chopped. Add to orange with sugar and lemon juice. Bring to a boil over medium-high heat, stirring constantly. Remove from heat; let cool. Cover and refrigerate for up to 4 days. Makes 1½ pints.

Summer Squash Relish

 When summer's bounty threatens to become summer's overabundance, pull out the kettle and turn some of the excess into this colorful relish. It's a crisp, sweet addition to franks or burgers.

 2½ **pounds zucchini or crookneck squash**
    1 **large onion**
    2 **medium-size carrots, cut into 1-inch chunks**
    1 **large green or red bell pepper, seeded**
 2½ **tablespoons salt**
 1½ **cups sugar**
 1¼ **cups white (distilled) vinegar**
 1½ **teaspoons *each* ground nutmeg and turmeric**
    1 **teaspoon celery seeds**
  ½ **teaspoon *each* dry mustard and pepper**

Insert metal blade. Chop zucchini as directed on page 15; transfer to a 6-quart kettle. Chop onion as directed on page 13; add to kettle. Place carrots in work bowl. Process, using on-off pulses, until chopped; add to kettle. Chop bell pepper as directed on page 15 and add to kettle. Pour in enough cold water to cover vegetables; stir in salt. Cover and refrigerate until next day.

Drain vegetables, rinse well, and drain again. Add sugar, vinegar, nutmeg, turmeric, celery seeds, mustard, and pepper. Simmer over medium heat, uncovered, until thick (30 to 40 minutes); stir frequently.

Fill hot sterilized canning jars with relish to within ¼ inch of rims. Wipe rims, then put hot sterilized lids and rings in place. Set jars on a rack in a large kettle and cover with boiling water. Bring water to a simmer; cook for 10 minutes. Makes about 3½ pints.

Pesto

 Originally, pesto was made with a mortar and pestle—hence its name (*pesto* means "pounded" in Italian). For today's cook, the processor whirls basil, cheese, and oil to a smooth paste in seconds.

    3 **ounces Parmesan cheese**
    1 **or 2 cloves garlic (optional)**
    2 **cups lightly packed fresh basil leaves**
      Olive oil

Insert metal blade. Grate cheese as directed on page 8 and set aside. Mince garlic (if used) as directed on page 13; leave in work bowl. Return cheese to work bowl and add basil. With motor running, pour ½ cup oil through feed tube and continue processing until incorporated. Use at once. Or, to store pesto, spoon it into small jars; then cover pesto in each jar with a thin layer of oil to prevent darkening. Refrigerate for up to 1 week; freeze for longer storage. Makes 1⅓ cups.

Pasta with Pesto

(Pictured on page 78)

To 4 cups hot, cooked packaged or fresh **fettuccine** (see page 79), spaghetti, or similar pasta (drained well), add 6 tablespoons **Pesto** and ¼ cup **butter** or margarine (softened). Toss gently to mix. Add 1 cup grated **Parmesan cheese** (see page 8) and toss to mix. Garnish with **pine nuts,** if desired. Offer additional cheese and Pesto at the table. Makes 4 to 6 servings.

Zucchini Pickles

Every gardener—and friend of a gardener—discovers at some point that zucchini can be prolific beyond belief. Use the surplus for these sweet, spiced pickles.

    5 pounds medium-size zucchini
    2 pounds medium-size white onions
    ¼ cup salt
      Ice water
    3 cloves garlic
    4 cups cider vinegar
    2 cups sugar
    1 tablespoon *each* celery seeds and turmeric
    2 tablespoons mustard seeds
    2 teaspoons ground ginger

Insert slicing disc. Slice zucchini as directed on page 15; transfer to a large mixing bowl. Slice onions as directed on page 13; add to zucchini, then stir in salt. Cover with ice water and let stand at room temperature for 1 to 2 hours. Drain, rinse well, and drain again.

Change to metal blade. Mince garlic as directed on page 13. Place garlic, vinegar, sugar, celery seeds, turmeric, mustard seeds, and gin-

ger in a 10 to 12-quart kettle. Bring to a boil over high heat, stirring. Boil, uncovered, for 2 to 3 minutes; stir in zucchini mixture, return to a boil, and boil for 2 more minutes.

Fill hot, sterilized jars with pickles and liquid to within ¼ inch of rims. Wipe rims, then put hot sterilized lids and rings in place. Let cool. Refrigerate any jars that don't seal. Makes 8 pints.

PROCESSING IN QUANTITY

When it comes time for making pickles and preserves, the processor can speed things up considerably. If used efficiently, it provides as much help as an extra pair of hands in the kitchen.

Organize the project. Before you peel the first peach, decide on the best order in which to process the ingredients (see "Recipe Conversion," page 53). Next, rinse all the ingredients called for; then peel, pit, seed, or hull as directed.

Since most recipes will require more than one work bowl's worth of chopping, have another large container handy to hold ingredients that have been processed. If all ingredients will eventually be cooked together (as in Pear & Ginger Chutney, facing page), transfer them directly to a pan or kettle of the size specified in the recipe.

Check capacity. As you work, take special care not to overload the work bowl. Refer to the manufacturer's directions to find the maximum capacity for your processor, and never exceed this recommendation. Overloading the work bowl only succeeds in producing uneven, unsatisfactory results.

Sweet Freezer Pickle Chips

◯ For the taste of homemade pickles without the trouble of canning, douse ice-cold cucumber and onion slices with hot syrup and freeze them. To serve, just thaw pickles overnight in the refrigerator.

2½ pounds cucumbers (about 5 medium-size)
1 medium-size white onion
2 tablespoons salt
   About 8 cups ice cubes
4 cups sugar
2 cups cider vinegar

Insert slicing disc. Slice cucumbers as directed on page 13; transfer to a large mixing bowl. Slice onion as directed on page 13. Add onion and salt to cucumbers; stir to mix. Cover with ice cubes and refrigerate for 2 to 3 hours.

Drain water from bowl and discard any unmelted ice cubes, but do not rinse cucumber mixture. Pack cucumber mixture in freezer containers or jars, filling each to within 1½ inches of rim.

In a 2 to 3-quart pan, combine sugar and vinegar. Bring to a boil over high heat, stirring until sugar is dissolved. Pour just enough hot syrup over cucumber mixture to cover. Put lids in place and freeze pickles for at least 1 week. Before serving, thaw in refrigerator for about 8 hours. Makes about 3 pints.

Garden Marinara Sauce

◯ When vine-ripened tomatoes are in abundance at summer's end, try this basil-seasoned fresh tomato sauce. It's wonderful over fresh pasta (see page 79); you might also use it in Peperonata (this page). Don't worry if you've made more than you can use right away—the sauce freezes beautifully.

1 cup lightly packed fresh basil leaves
3 or 4 cloves garlic
3 large onions
6 pounds ripe tomatoes, peeled, cored, and quartered (no need to seed)
¼ cup olive oil
½ to 1 tablespoon sugar
   Salt and pepper

Insert metal blade. Chop basil as directed for parsley on page 15; set aside. Mince garlic as directed on page 13 and leave in work bowl. Chop onions as directed on page 13; set onions and garlic aside. Chop tomatoes as directed on page 15.

Heat oil in a 6 to 8-quart kettle over medium heat. Add onions and garlic and cook, stirring frequently, until onions are golden brown (about 20 minutes). Add tomatoes and basil and cook, uncovered, stirring occasionally to prevent sticking, until sauce is reduced to 8 cups (45 minutes to 1 hour). Add sugar, then season to taste with salt and pepper.

To store sauce, cover and refrigerate for up to 1 week; or package airtight and freeze for up to 6 months. Bring to a boil before using. Makes about 2 quarts.

Peperonata

◯◯ Peperonata is a saucy relish made from sliced sweet peppers and homemade marinara sauce. It's a nice accompaniment for grilled meats or poultry, and just as good as a dip for butter lettuce leaves, pocket bread wedges, or crisp plain crackers. It also makes a colorful addition to an antipasto platter.

About 10 assorted sweet peppers (such as red or green bell peppers or sweet yellow peppers)
2 large onions
2 cloves garlic
¼ cup olive oil
2½ cups Garden Marinara Sauce (this page)
   Salt and pepper

Insert slicing disc. Following directions on pages 15 and 13, slice peppers and set aside (you should have about 8 cups); then slice onions and set aside. Change to metal blade and mince garlic as directed on page 13.

Heat oil in a 12 to 14-inch frying pan over medium heat. Add onions and cook, stirring occasionally, until soft (about 5 minutes). Add garlic, peppers, and Garden Marinara Sauce; then cover and cook until peppers are tender when pierced (8 to 10 minutes). Season to taste with salt and pepper.

Let cool to room temperature, then serve. Or cover and refrigerate for up to 1 week; or package airtight and freeze for up to 6 months (thaw before using). Serve cold or at room temperature. Makes about 4 pints.

Spiced German Mustard

When you make your own mustard, you can control the degree of puréeing to make a condiment with as coarse or fine a texture as you like. Our spicy mustard is made with the white (yellow) mustard seeds widely sold in supermarket spice sections.

The concentration of the seasoned vinegar mixture determines the mustard's pungency; if you reduce it by half (as we suggest here), you'll get a medium-hot mustard. For a hotter product, reduce the mixture further.

- ⅓ cup white (yellow) mustard seeds
- ¼ cup dry mustard
- ½ cup cold water
- 2 cloves garlic
- 1 small onion
- 1 cup cider vinegar
- 2 tablespoons firmly packed brown sugar
- 1 teaspoon salt
- ½ teaspoon ground cinnamon
- ¼ teaspoon *each* ground allspice, dill seeds, and dry tarragon
- ⅛ teaspoon turmeric
- 1 to 2 tablespoons honey

In a bowl, stir together mustard seeds, dry mustard, and water. Let stand for at least 3 hours.

Insert metal blade. Mince garlic as directed on page 13; leave in work bowl. Chop onion as directed on page 13.

Place onion and garlic in a small noncorrosive pan and add vinegar, sugar, salt, cinnamon, allspice, dill seeds, tarragon, and turmeric. Simmer over medium heat, uncovered, until reduced by about half (10 to 15 minutes); then pour through a wire strainer into mustard mixture.

Place mixture in work bowl. Process, using on-off pulses, until puréed to the desired consistency. Pour into the top of a double boiler; cook over simmering water, stirring occasionally, until thickened (10 to 15 minutes; mustard will thicken a bit more as it cools). Stir in honey. Let cool; then cover and refrigerate for at least 3 days before using. (Mustard keeps for up to 2 years.) Makes about 1 cup.

Apricot Leather

Fruit leather is a sweet, nutritious snack that's also fun to eat. You make a smooth purée of fresh fruit and sugar, then spread it on baking sheets and set it in a low oven to dry. After about 8 hours, you'll have soft, chewy sheets of "leather" to tear into strips and eat out of hand.

- 2 pounds apricots, quartered and pitted
- 6 to 8 tablespoons sugar
- 2 tablespoons lemon juice

Insert metal blade. Place apricots, 6 tablespoons of the sugar, and lemon juice in work bowl, half at a time (or all at once in a large-capacity processor); process continuously until puréed. Taste and add up to 2 more tablespoons sugar. Line two 10 by 15-inch rimmed baking pans with plastic wrap; spoon half the purée into each lined pan and spread evenly over bottom with a rubber spatula.

Place pans in a 150° oven (or oven set on "warm"), allowing at least 4 inches drying space between oven racks. Dry for 6 to 8 hours or until leather is firm and feels dry. Remove plastic and leather from pans; roll up together while still warm and twist ends of plastic to seal. Wrap each roll in additional plastic wrap. Store at room temperature for up to 1 month or freeze for up to 1 year. Makes 2 rolls.

Peach or Nectarine Leather

Follow directions for **Apricot Leather,** but substitute 2 pounds **yellow freestone peaches** or nectarines, peeled, quartered, and pitted, for apricots. (If using nectarines, do not peel.)

Plum Leather

Follow directions for **Apricot Leather,** but substitute 2 pounds firm-fleshed **plums,** quartered and pitted, for apricots. Omit lemon juice.

Strawberry Leather

Follow directions for **Apricot Leather,** but substitute 2 pints **strawberries** (hulled) for apricots. Decrease sugar to 4 to 6 tablespoons.

Index

Metric Conversion Table

To change	To	Multiply by
ounces (oz.)	grams (g)	28
pounds (lbs.)	kilograms (kg)	0.45
teaspoons	milliliters (ml)	5
tablespoons	milliliters (ml)	15
fluid ounces (fl. oz.)	milliliters (ml)	30
cups	liters (l)	0.24
pints (pt.)	liters (l)	0.47
quarts (qt.)	liters (l)	0.95
gallons (gal.)	liters (l)	3.8
Fahrenheit temperature(°F)	Celsius temperature (°C)	5/9 after subtracting 32